HOW MANY

AMERICANS?

HOW MANY AMERICANS?

POPULATION, IMMIGRATION *and the* ENVIRONMENT

LEON F. BOUVIER

and

LINDSEY GRANT

SIERRA CLUB BOOKS   SAN FRANCISCO

This project was sponsored by the Center for Immigration Studies with the support of the Compton Foundation and the Frank Weeden Foundation. The Center for Immigration Studies is a nonprofit organization founded in 1985 to conduct research and policy analysis and disseminate information on immigration trends and the economic, social, demographic, and environmental impacts of immigration. Based in Washington, D.C., the Center maintains an active publishing program, including a quarterly journal, regular background papers, and books and monographs.

The Sierra Club, founded in 1892 by John Muir, has devoted itself to the study and protection of the earth's scenic and ecological resources—mountains, wetlands, woodlands, wild shores and rivers, deserts and plains. The publishing program of the Sierra Club offers books to the public as a nonprofit educational service in the hope that they may enlarge the public's understanding of the Club's basic concerns. The point of view expressed in each book, however, does not necessarily represent that of the Club. The Sierra Club has some sixty chapters coast to coast, in Canada, Hawaii, and Alaska. For information about how you may participate in its programs to preserve wilderness and the quality of life, please address inquiries to Sierra Club, 730 Polk Street, San Francisco, CA 94109.

Library of Congress Cataloging-in-Publication Data

Bouvier, Leon F.
    How many Americans? : population, immigration, and the
environment / Leon F. Bouvier and Lindsey Grant.
        p.   cm.
    Includes bibliographical references and index.
    ISBN 0-87156-385-1
    1. Population forecasting—United States. 2. Population—
Environmental aspects—United States. 3. United States—
Emigration and immigration—Social aspects. I. Grant, Lindsey.
II. Title.
HB3505.B67   1994
304.6'0973—dc20   94-6163

Production by Susan Ristow
Cover design by Big Fish Books, San Francisco
Book design by Christine Taylor
Illustrations by Elaine B. Dawson
Composition by Wilsted & Taylor
Printed in the United States of America on acid-free paper
containing a minimum of 50% recovered waste paper,
of which at least 10% of the fiber content is post-consumer waste

10   9   8   7   6   5   4   3   2   1

CONTENTS

TABLES

FIGURES

ACKNOWLEDGMENTS

In preparing this book, we received valuable advice and suggestions from many colleagues. David Simcox, former executive director of the Center for Immigration Studies, was instrumental in getting the project off the ground. George High, the present executive director of the center, was particularly helpful, as were staff members Jessica Vaughan, Jack Martin, and Rosemary Jenks.

The earlier work of many scholars made this book possible. Special thanks go to those who prepared papers for Lindsey Grant's *Elephants in the Volkswagen* (1992), many of which are cited herein. Donald Mann, who first published these papers, deserves a very special thank you.

Over the years numerous citizens, not necessarily scientists, have expressed concern over the relationship between population growth and the environment. We have benefited greatly from the insights of Vice President Al Gore and former Ambassador George Kennan.

Elaine Dawson did all the word processing necessary to put the manuscript into final shape. Her expertise and cooperation were both deeply appreciated.

A very special thank you goes to the Compton Foundation and the Frank Weeden Foundation for supporting this project. Not only were the foundations very generous, they were also patient with us as we tried to meet agreed-upon deadlines.

We thank our respective spouses, Terri and Burwell. Without their support and understanding, it would have been much more difficult to complete this book.

Finally, we thank Barbara Ras, our editor at Sierra Club Books. Barbara was especially helpful with her many suggestions that greatly enhanced the final product. Carl Pope,

Judith Kunofsky, and Ernest Callenbach all read various drafts and made worthwhile comments.

Of course, the final product reflects our opinions solely and does not necessarily reflect those of the Compton Foundation, the Frank Weeden Foundation, the Sierra Club, the Center for Immigration Studies, or the many friends who were kind enough to offer suggestions.

HOW MANY

AMERICANS?

INTRODUCTION

In South India, at a certain festival, it was customary to roll out a giant ceremonial chariot in honor of Lord Vishnu. The chariot was wheeled, but no provision was made for steering it. Pulled and pushed by devotees in religious ecstasy, it crushed everything in its path: people, animals, buildings. It was called the Juggernaut.

Population growth in the United States has something of that same terrible appearance of inevitability. Yet like the Juggernaut, it is driven, not by fate, but by humans unconcerned about the consequences of its progress. If we can bring those driving the population Juggernaut to consider the consequences of what they are doing, perhaps we can turn it from its present destructive course. That is the purpose of this book.

The first evidence of population growth is crowding. It is inescapable to those who dwell in the metropolitan areas of this country, confronted with rising crime and teeming streets, snarled traffic, the pall of air pollution, the degeneration of the cities as civilized places to live and the difficulty of escaping into a less degraded countryside. The air pollution is apparent also to the country dweller, who sees the haze stretching outward from the urban areas. On a bad day, the residents of the Owens Valley can see the air pollution from Los Angeles, 300 miles away. They have other evidence of the penalties of urban growth, since Los Angeles long ago took their water. Those are the obvious signs, but they are only superficial indicators of fundamental and disturbing directions in which population growth is driving the nation.

The population Juggernaut is not easily stopped, and the effort to do so conflicts with deeply held feelings about privacy, the role of government in our society and the right of

1

people to do their own thing. Moreover, there are only two ways of stopping population growth: lower immigration, lower fertility, or more realistically, both. In the present political climate in America, one could hardly select two more explosive topics. There is a new generation that takes seriously the fact that we live on a shared planet and that "all persons are siblings" (to update the Chinese proverb into a "politically correct" and nonsexist formula). To many people under 30, it would seem, an "alien" comes from outer space, not from Mexico. For that generation, and those of their elders who are tuned in, any proposal to limit immigration conjures up images of racists and skinheads. The debate is thus plunged into a region of moral absolutes, where to compromise is to sin. Any proposal to limit immigration generates charges of "xenophobia" or the allegation that the authors are trying to preserve a privileged position for the United States in a desperately poor world.

Any proposal to limit fertility encounters hostility from two directions. On one side, it is met with the charge of "racism," since minorities tend to have higher fertility than Whites. From another quarter, right-to-lifers equate family planning with abortion, which they regard as evil. (In this heated atmosphere, the thought is not entertained that family planning may in fact forestall abortions.) They do not examine the demographic consequences of their viewpoint.

The argument that controlling immigration is morally inadmissible is a serious one, even though it is frequently presented in intemperate language. We will address it at the close of this introduction.[1] For the moment, however, the point is that, if those critics of limited immigration or a fertility policy accept the argument that U.S. population growth is destroying the environment, they become caught in a moral dilemma. There is a conflict between the pursuit of valid but conflicting objectives. The moral duty to succor the desperate foreigner necessarily conflicts with the duty to pass on an undiminished heritage to our descendants.

One way out of that dilemma is denial, the refusal to admit that there is a U.S. population problem. Those who

2

choose to escape the dilemma by this route may argue that the nation's problems are solvable on their own terms— that more freeways will handle the traffic and more money for education and law enforcement will reduce the crime, that technical fixes can control air and water pollution, and that so long as there are oceans one can obtain enough fresh water from desalinization.

The time is long past for such compartmentalized efforts at solutions. The times are out of kilter, and most of our problems are driven by population growth, technological change and, in the United States, high individual rates of consumption. The very success of the modern industrial economies is generating changes that in turn threaten, not just the successes we have achieved, but the natural systems that, little appreciated by us, support these economies and the artificial world in which most of us live.

Even without population growth, our nation's voracious consumptive appetite is a problem. But population growth exacerbates the problem, and the more rapid (and unplanned) that growth, the more damaging it is.

The messages in this book are really quite straightforward. First, the human race is a part of the natural ecosystem of the Earth, not a privileged superspecies given "the earth as [its] inheritance."[2] Second, the disturbances caused by human activities have accelerated so dramatically in this half-century, driven by population growth and the technological explosion, that they threaten not only the continuation of a way of life that we have come to take for granted, but perhaps even the continuation of life systems as we understand them. Third, the United States, because of its size and consumption habits, is the most destabilizing unit of the vast ecosystem we call the Earth; moreover, present migration and fertility patterns will only strengthen that destabilizing influence in the next half-century or more. And fourth, the means for controlling and reversing these terrible forces lie within our hands, if only as a society we can be wise enough to understand and employ them.

Simple as this sounds, it will take a profound reordering

3

of our society's philosophical underpinnings, and some very difficult practical political decisions, to carry out such a program.

The population issue, as we see it, is a double one: rapid and unplanned growth itself has high costs and detrimental effects on the quality of life of all humans; and the resultant numbers—the sheer size of the populations that have resulted from that growth—put intolerable strains on the environment that supports us.

Whenever the carrying capacity of any region is surpassed, living conditions deteriorate. By carrying capacity, we mean the number of individuals that can be supported without degrading the physical, cultural and social environment—that is, without reducing the ability of the environment to sustain the desired living conditions over the long term. Decent living conditions mean different things to different people. To us, they mean utilizing resources rationally rather than contributing to their depletion, breathing fresh rather than contaminated air, having a sufficient amount of clean, unpolluted water. They mean having decent transportation, health and education services. They mean safe streets and a feeling of personal security.

There is a tradeoff between population size and the standard of living. One can envisage a populous economy (though it would be hard to name one) that is within its carrying capacity, but at such a low level of individual consumption that the standard of living is constrained—a China or India with better environmental practices. At the other extreme, one may imagine a society built on the much-maligned automobile, where every potential driver has a car to suit his or her taste and yet the environment is not threatened. The only requirement in that scenario is that there can be very few cars, and therefore very few people.

Given current population growth in the United States, we wonder how crowded our country will be in the future. Will its highways become intolerable? Will we still be able to enjoy its beautiful beaches and wilderness areas, or will visitors risk being trampled by hordes of people all trying to enjoy the nation's bounties? More important, will our farmlands, forests and aquifers be able to support the numbers of people? Will the continuing rise of economic activity imperil the atmosphere and waters of our country? Will human activity lead to climate change that displaces and diminishes agricultural production? Will it lead to rising sea levels and coastal flooding? Finally, and in the worst case, will the pollution generated by the rising curve of human activity threaten terrestrial life-support systems and eventually even human life?

The question is given immediacy by two connected phenomena. First, the rate of economic activity in the United States and in the world has accelerated remarkably in this half-century, and the resulting effluvia and wastes have begun to overwhelm natural systems as never before in human history. Second, this activity has been built on petroleum, and petroleum is now the first major mineral resource facing imminent depletion. The United States, the erstwhile USSR and Saudi Arabia were the most richly endowed oil producers on Earth. Unlike the other two, the United States has already run through more than half its resources. With only a few years' supply left, we are growing more dependent on imports in a tightening market and with a serious balance-of-payments problem already upon us. The combination of rising environmental costs, rising energy demand and a shrinking resource base promises that the energy transition the United States must go through in the next generation or so will likely be the most abrupt and expensive economic transformation that any nation has ever undertaken. We need to be asking the question: How does this looming adjustment relate to our national policies that continue to encourage population growth?

Most observers agree that there are limits to population growth, as there are to any material growth on a finite planet. Some may feel that future U.S. growth should be limited, with an end in sight within the next century. Others are convinced that even today's population of 250 million is too large, that the United States is already overpopulated. In this book, we argue the latter position.

Curiously, many people concerned about the environmental effects of population growth think the solution lies solely in reducing fertility. But populations grow or contract because of shifts in three basic demographic variables: fertility, mortality and migration. If population growth is to be contained and eventually ended, all three variables must be considered.

It is true, of course, that for many years high fertility was the main contributor to population growth in the United States. Throughout the baby boom era, from 1947 to 1964, women in this country averaged between three and four births. Indeed, that growth rate gave rise to the "zero population growth" (ZPG) movement, founded by biologist Paul Ehrlich. If women would average only 2.1 children, it was thought, the nation would cease growing.

By 1972, the 2.1 barrier had been broken; in fact, for the next fifteen or so years American fertility hovered around 1.8 live births per woman. Yet the population continued to grow more rapidly than anywhere else in the industrialized world. Obviously, something besides fertility was contributing to such growth.

That "something" was immigration.

It is ironic that at about the time the ZPG movement was gathering steam in the mid-1960s, new legislation passed in 1965 and put into effect in 1968 led to a massive increase in immigration to the United States. The magic 2.1 number clearly did not take immigration into consideration, perhaps in part because the numbers of newcomers were quite low during the 1950s and most of the 1960s. Not taking immigration into account, it turned out, was a serious error.

Even with limited immigration, 2.1 was never the correct goal for replacement-level fertility. As long as there is any net immigration, zero population growth (i.e., where fertility and immigration equal mortality and emigration) can be achieved only through a combination of below-replacement-level fertility and specified immigration levels.[3]

However, the population size when zero growth is reached can be astronomical if the fertility is just below replacement and immigration is high. Later, we will discuss the various scenarios that would allow the nation's population to cease growing through combinations of below-replacement fertility and various levels of immigration.

In the struggle to balance population size and a sustainable environment, only two paths can be taken. Either we can adopt reasonable population policies that will ensure a reduction in and an eventual end to growth, or we can do nothing and constantly try to adjust every aspect of life to increased numbers of people. Speaking about the planet, but using words that are certainly applicable to the situation in the United States, then-Senator Al Gore put it well:

> Do we have so much faith in our own adaptability that we will risk destroying the integrity of the entire global system? If we try to adapt to the changes we are causing rather than prevent them in the first place, have we made an appropriate choice? Can we understand how much destruction this choice might finally cause?[4]

In the following chapters we will first examine the connections between population growth and the environmental, resource and social issues that already confront the nation. We will then project population patterns for the United States in the twenty-first century, if present demographic patterns continue and if the nation does nothing about them. We will also look at how such a rate of growth and eventual population size will affect the environmental and social problems already confronting us. In effect, we will try to answer the question: What are the consequences of doing nothing about population growth?

Assuming that most Americans would prefer to do something about population growth before it is too late, we will explore alternative population scenarios as well. Our purpose is to illustrate the need to consider all three demographic variables—fertility, mortality and immigration—if population growth is to be stopped. In particular, lower fertility coupled with various levels of immigration will be examined. We will also offer suggestions on how fertility might be reduced and immigration controlled.

Finally, we will speculate on what kind of society would emerge—economically, politically and socially—under a no-growth scenario, and we will describe what seem to us certain preconditions, involving social behavior and the nation's view of itself, if our society is ever to come to grips with the population issue and attempt to steer the direction of future change.

Readers with a broad view of the Earth may ask why we argue for limiting immigration, when one person more in this country means one person less in another place where conditions are probably more desperate than they are here. Our answer is that we recognize this to be an urgent *world* problem. If we had our way, we would carry our message to the third world as well, where it would be about fertility, not migration. (Population growth, at least until the recent spurt of immigration in Europe, is under control in most industrial nations other than the United States.) We believe that third world efforts to control their population growth are probably the most important national project that those countries could be pursuing. It is important to our future well-being, as to theirs, just as they have an interest in U.S. efforts to control pollution in a shared world. Family planning funding should be the highest single priority for U.S. foreign aid, rather than an afterthought that has amounted in recent years to only about 2 percent of total U.S. aid.[5] The United States should actively support those international proposals and projects that help third world countries to lift their economies, improve the status of women, provide better education and institute the medical and social reforms that provide the framework for fertility reduction.

However, there is a drawback in preaching to the distant: their decisions, finally, are theirs, not ours. The United

States can help them only if they want the help. At home, we have both the responsibility and the power to address our own population problem. It is to our fellow citizens, therefore, that we address this book.

This is a classic example of the environmentalists' injunction to "think globally, act locally." The population issue must be addressed in every country where it exists, and while we should do what we can to help others, our problem is at home.

The United States cannot solve the third world population problem by absorbing it, even if we were to accept the prospect of becoming as crowded as India. World population growth in this decade alone will be almost one billion, almost all of it in the third world—with almost another billion in the next decade, and the next. No matter how vaulting our hubris, we cannot hope to resolve a problem of that scale alone. We can, however, do the world a service by putting our own house in order, because per capita we generate so much of the world's pollution. We are also the world's largest food exporter. During the Indian drought of 1967, we supplied about one-third of the wheat that Indians ate that year. We do not particularly help others if we come to eat our own surplus, and need more.

The argument against limiting immigration rests on the assumption that the nation has an a priori commitment to the relief of others. The argument is thoroughly altruistic and springs from the best of intentions. However, in the absence of evidence that we can in fact provide that relief, it offers the prospect of sacrifice without the prospect of much gain for others. It is an argument that is peculiarly American, and rooted probably in a rather narrow section of the middle class. It is also rather one-sided. Somehow, it seems easier to become morally indignant in support of the rights of the immigrant than of disenfranchised Americans. The poor, who feel the pinch, are not so altruistic. One opinion poll after another reveals overwhelming support among Americans, including minorities, for the proposition that immigration should be reduced. In one in-depth survey of

Hispanic groups in 1992, majorities ranging from 66 to 79 percent stated that immigration is already too high.[6]

The more general assumption, worldwide, is that nations are entitled to pursue their self-interest. The element we would add is that it should be enlightened self-interest, based on the recognition that national behavior is not a zero-sum game. We all share the Earth with each other, and indeed with all living creatures.

It is a choice that each person must make alone. We hope that those not willing to concede the legitimacy of action to protect the national inheritance will read this book. There are compelling arguments for the ideal of a sustainable society, in the context of a sustainable world.

The argument that limiting fertility is racism is quickly disposed of. As figure 4.1 (chapter 4) makes clear, fertility is correlated more closely with education and income than with race. In a 1990 survey, for example, Black college-educated women had lower fertility than Whites or Hispanics. The fertility goal advocated in this book can be stated simply as "stop at two." If substantially all women, rich or poor, educated or uneducated, were to have no more than two children, fertility would drop enough to achieve a population rollback. With smaller cohorts entering the job market, the chances would improve for the children of the poor to establish a career and climb out of poverty. This seems a humane objective at both the personal and demographic level.

On that note, let us begin the task of giving substance to the generalizations in this introduction.

1

POPULATION

AND ENVIRONMENT

Believing ourselves to be separate from the earth means having no idea how we fit into the natural cycle of life and no understanding of the natural processes of change that affect us and that we in turn are affecting. It means that we attempt to chart the course of our civilization by reference to ourselves alone. No wonder we are lost and confused. No wonder so many people feel their lives are wasted. Our species used to flourish within the intricate and interdependent web of life, but we have chosen to leave the garden. Unless we find a way to dramatically change our civilization and our way of thinking about the relationship between humankind and the earth, our children will inherit a wasteland.

Al Gore, *Earth in the Balance: Ecology and the Human Spirit*

GLOBAL CHANGE AND THE U.S. ROLE

Homo sapiens is a very recent, very talented and thoroughly disruptive species. We are perhaps the principal source of change to the Earth's ecosystem—most of it unintentional—and the pace of our disruption is increasing. The rate at which the species is altering the Earth has accelerated geometrically. Arguably, the most important fact about this century is the intertwined growth of human populations and human technology and the resultant changes to the Earth and to human society.

Figure 1.1 tracks human population growth and several key human activities during the twentieth century. (Energy consumption is expressed in millions of barrels per day of oil equivalent; introduction of chemicals into the environment in absolute numbers; and cereal production, fishery harvest and fertilizer production in millions of metric tons, the last calculated in terms of the basic nutrients nitrogen, phosphorus and potassium.)

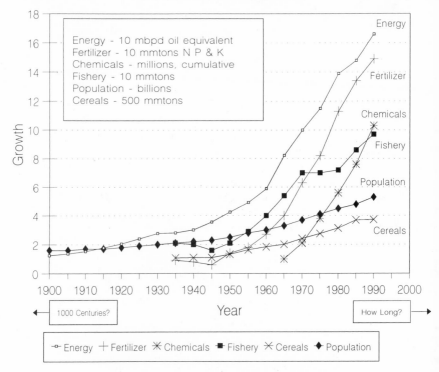

FIGURE 1.1 *Change: The Wild Century*

Perhaps the most dramatic thing about figure 1.1 is the lower left corner. In all humankind's time on the Earth—from 1,000 to 10,000 centuries, depending on what one accepts as the starting point for the species—we had reached only the low levels of economic activity shown for 1900. In this one brief century, and particularly in its second half, there has been an utterly unprecedented explosion of human activity. We think of the "population explosion"—and the quadrupling anticipated in this century certainly deserves the name—but the population curve manages to look rather modest compared with the increases in energy, fertilizers and particularly chemicals that have supported that population growth. The fundamental question posed by the graph is: What are the consequences of such growth?

There is a simple little riddle: "If there are a dozen water lilies in a pond, doubling daily, and they cover the pond in 30 days, when was the pond half covered?" The answer, of course, is on the 29th day. The expansion of human activities on the Earth resembles the story of that pond, as will become clear later in this book. The explosive growth of inputs into agriculture and industry is altering our habitat. We humans have been introducing new combinations of chemicals and elements—compounds of mercury, lead, hydrocarbons, chlorine, and on and on—into the biosystem unlike anything it has borne before. We are introducing more familiar things such as nitrogen and carbon compounds at an unprecedented rate.

These disturbances are having profound effects on the world around us. Acid rain. Climate change. Too little ozone in the stratosphere and too much at ground level. The destruction of life forms at a rate that has been compared to the Cretaceous extinctions. The rapid loss of forests under the double onslaught of overharvesting and environmental damage. Farmland destruction and desertification. Perhaps even more ominous, we do not really know what we are doing. Of the 11 million chemicals registered by the Chemical Abstract Service, some 60,000 are in regular commercial use. Of these, very few have been tested for primary health effects,[1] to say nothing of the multiple consequences as they break down, combine and move through the ecosystem.

Even many environmentalists may think of these disruptions simply as threatening rather remote good things, like caribou herds in Alaska, or creating unpleasant conditions like smog or crowding that degrade the quality of life. Certainly, the changes are having such effects, and others such as the social collapse of our cities, but the issue may be graver than the bland term "quality of life" suggests. Humanity is on a course that, if continued, could threaten our own survival.

There has been much debate about "growth/collapse"

cycles. The Earth is remarkably resilient, and nobody really knows how much abuse it can take, but the human tribe seems intent on testing the limits. Civilizations have over-stretched their limits before, and collapsed, leading to population declines. The dangers of the course humankind has embarked upon are not simply the imaginings of zealots. Witness the unprecedented joint warning in 1992 by the officers of the U.S. National Academy of Sciences (NAS) and the Royal Society of London:

> If current predictions of population growth prove accurate and patterns of human activity on the planet remain unchanged, science and technology may not be able to prevent either irreversible degradation of the environment or continued poverty for much of the world.[2]

Or the somber and eloquently phrased rumination by Daniel Koshland, editor of *Science* magazine, that we must "curb our primordial instinct to increase replication of our own species at the expense of others because the global ecology is threatened. So ask not whether the bell tolls for the owl or the whale or the rhinoceros; it tolls for us."[3] Scientists understand connections that politicians so far have generally hoped to ignore. We have been warned.

What do these gloomy speculations have to do with the specific issue of U.S. population? The United States is a major part of the global problem. If the total human population is quadrupling in this century, the United States is not far behind; we have *more than* trebled. We are the third largest nation on Earth and, because of our consumption-intensive way of living, the leading source of some of the most immediate threats to the future of humankind: climate warming, acid precipitation and the loss of stratospheric ozone. We contribute to species impoverishment by altering habitat and cutting down our remaining old forests, and our demand for timber, along with that of the other industrial nations, hastens the destruction of tropical forests.

We Americans are not just degrading the globe; we are the victims of our own behavior.

THE STATISTICS OF DEGRADATION

The way the country runs its affairs right now, most of our economic activity is not sustainable. One can reel off a catalog of the problems we are generating:

U.S. behavior is continuing to generate *acid precipitation* and *climate change.*

The Earth has lost about 3 percent of its protective stratospheric ozone, resulting in a 6 percent rise in *ultraviolet radiation.* Another 3 percent loss is expected by 2000.[4]

Americans each year draw 25 percent more water from *groundwater* resources than gets replaced by nature. Falling water tables have already curtailed irrigation from some aquifers, and the competition for water between irrigated agriculture and urban population growth has already led to the systematic diversion of water from agriculture to cities in Arizona and California.

Erosion is costing the United States about 3 billion tons of *topsoil* per year.

We are cutting down the last of our old-growth *forests,* out of greed, and we will soon have to rely on sterile tree plantations for lumber. Our destruction of forests raises serious questions about the rate at which we are prepared to wipe out other ecosystems and species.

Our agriculture and household wastes are poisoning the *wetlands* and wiping out our *coastal fishery.*[5]

Our cities generate twice as much *solid waste* as they did in 1960,[6] and the problem of disposal is critical. Because they were polluting, or simply full, the number of landfills declined from 20,000 in 1978 to 6,000 in 1990, and more than half the remainder will be closed by mid-decade.[7] Cities have unsuccessfully tried to unload the waste on third world countries. They have tried incineration, and it in turn generated serious environmental hazards. Major eastern cities have been negotiating with rural counties as far away as New Mexico and Texas to accept the stuff. The nation is on a treadmill. Recycling is one legitimate approach, but hardly the final one. Even in Japan, which has necessarily adopted an aggressive waste recycling program, the best programs recycle only 50 percent of the waste. The problem must be attacked at the roots: first, population growth; and second, our national consumption habits.

We cannot figure out what to do with *sewage sludge.* Coastal cities regularly pump it to sea. Faced with polluted beaches, New York City tried to dump it farther out, only to imperil the offshore fishery. In a simpler age, the sludge would have been good fertilizer, but it is now contaminated with heavy metals and toxins. The Carson sewage treatment plant serving the Los Angeles area actually has a permit to pump sewage including lead and mercury—two thoroughly dangerous substances—into Santa Monica Bay.[8]

The nation generates over 13 billion tons of waste each year (including mine tailings), or 50 tons per person. Of that, about 2 percent is identified as *hazardous waste.* Laws have been passed to control its disposal (and have consequently led to a dramatic increase in clandestine dumping). Current dumping is only part of the problem. The nation has a legacy of wastes left from the era of reckless industrial activity, when it was simply assumed that one could dump them into the environment. Superfund was created to clean up those toxic industrial waste sites, but it has access to funds totalling only $15 billion for a task of heroic but unknown magnitude. More than 33,000 potential sites have been identified; of these, the Superfund administrators have ruled out federal action on 19,000. They have further identified a National Priorities List of 1,245 sites, on 550 of which they have begun long-term remedial work. In other words, the work, even on the identified sites, has just begun, and the final bill is incalculable. We don't really know the scale of the problem. Records of earlier dumping are scanty or nonexistent. The current rate of illegal dumping to avoid the cost of proper disposal is unknown.

Moreover, toxic wastes do their damage largely by polluting groundwater supplies, on which about half the U.S.

population depends for its drinking water. The damage takes time as chemicals work their way toward the water table, and there is no way of knowing exactly what toxic chemicals are already on their way from leaking chemical drums, nearly 2 million buried gas station tanks, and other miscellaneous tanks around the nation that are not even subject to regulation. In sum, the problem of toxic wastes presents a huge but unknown bill for cleaning up past poisoning and preventing its continuation.

We haven't figured out how to handle *nuclear wastes,* while our inventory of spent fuel in temporary (and dangerous) storage has risen from 55 tons in 1970 to about 18,000 tons in 1988.[9] It may cost more than $100 billion to clean up sites such as Hanford, Rocky Flats and the Savannah River facility, with no assurance that the job can be done.

We are living on *fossil fuels* that won't last. Our total national resources of petroleum probably equal less than 16 years' current consumption. Yet we keep on using petroleum as if there were no tomorrow.

We have only 10 percent more road mileage than we had in 1960—because the basic road network was already in place—but we have 150 percent more vehicles using the roads.[10] Look again at the disparity between those two figures. The country didn't need new roads; it needed more lanes and more cloverleaf intersections to avoid choking on the *increasing traffic.* Despite a road improvement program that includes the Interstate network, the largest peacetime capital project in U.S. history, the nation falls behind. Traffic gets worse every year, and automobiles rank as our primary source of pollution. Florida provides a dramatic example. In the 1980s alone, despite the highway construction, the number of registered vehicles per lane-mile of highway increased 28 percent—largely because of population growth.[11]

Unemployment averaged 4.6 percent in the 1960s. It rose to 7.2 percent in the 1980s. This figure does not take into account the rising number, particularly of young people, who have simply dropped out of the labor market or who have part-time jobs for lack of permanent ones.[12]

As these unhappy examples were cited, we could have repeated the refrain that, if the population had stopped growing in 1950, each of those problems would be much smaller than it now is, because U.S. population has grown by two-thirds in that period. Rather than reciting the litany, however, let us state the general principle. As a rule of thumb, the relationship between environment (or resources) and population can be described like this:

$$Impact\ (on\ resources\ \&\ environment) =$$
$$Population \times Consumption\ Levels \times Technology$$

or

$$I = PCT$$

The formula is not absolute. There are "thresholds" and "non-linearities." In other words, the impact may not always rise in a straight line. Nevertheless, it is a good way of looking at the connections; and where there are nonlinear impacts, they tend to be worse than the linear ones.

Let us flesh out these generalizations by taking a closer look at five of the key population/environmental issues that we presently face and that may be central to our future well-being: the social problems felt most acutely in our biggest cities, energy, forests, agriculture and biodiversity. The choice and the order may seem arbitrary, but they are not. They proceed from immediate and palpable issues to ones that may seem remote but which over time may be the most fundamental. All of them are connected, sometimes in unexpected ways.

THE BREAKDOWN OF THE CITIES

The interplay between population and the environment is not confined to the natural environment. The 1992 riots in Los Angeles represent a good case study of the connections

18

between demography, policy and the future of the cities. The tensions that led to the Rodney King beating and the subsequent explosion of violence, tensions between the police and the populace and between ethnic groups, reflect a society very much on edge. The causes for the violence were complex, and we are probably still too close to understand them fully, but demographic change was certainly a factor—yet it was almost completely ignored in the postriot commentary.

A central point of this example is that the rate and direction of change may be as important as the total numbers. Los Angeles, a sprawling city, is not particularly densely populated. The problem is the explosive combination of growing numbers of alienated and unskilled youth confronted with an influx of newcomers—in this case, immigrants—that makes their situation more hopeless. Immigration and fertility are (along with mortality) the demographic variables that determine population growth. When they are high—as in Los Angeles—they generate massive population growth (the Los Angeles metropolitan area has gone from 6 to 14 million people since 1960) and intense social frictions.

In the 1960s, the nation set out on perhaps its greatest moral crusade: to bring Blacks into the economic and social mainstream. There were problems to begin with, and national policies made them worse. The crusade began at a tough time, when particularly large cohorts of young people—the postwar baby boomers—were entering the job market. Jobs had to be created, initially at the unskilled level, just as the technological revolution—which continues today—was drying up the demand for unskilled labor. Moreover, the social revolution unleashed by World War II that had caused young women to pour into the paid labor force was gathering momentum. Competition for jobs was tough indeed.

How did the nation respond? It didn't.

Just as the crusade to bring Blacks into the mainstream

began, the country embarked on the interstate highway program. One result was to facilitate White flight (and middle-class flight generally) to the suburbs as poor Blacks continued their historic migration from farms to cities. The cities were thus effectively resegregated, the poor Blacks were isolated, the cities' tax base eroded, and there went both the social contact and the financial resources to educate poor young Blacks and help them to join the rest of the society. Busing was hardly a solution when the middle class lived in different educational jurisdictions and was fighting to preserve its own schools.

Even more important, the federal government, through its policies on immigration and fertility, *increased* the competition for unskilled jobs rather than trying to limit it. Every immigration "reform" of the past two decades has raised legal immigration. Moreover, the "family reunification" bias of U.S. immigration policy has encouraged the immigration of the unskilled, who compete with our own unskilled, especially minorities and earlier immigrants. Because of some employers' demands for cheap labor, the government has failed to enforce the immigration laws we have, and this has encouraged illegal immigration. The *New York Times* called it the "policy of the wink." The Census Bureau counted a net influx of 2.3 million foreigners into California in the 1980s, and that does not include the illegal immigrants who chose not to be counted. Los Angeles's Hispanic population increased 70 percent in the 1980s. The Asian population increased 74 percent. The already fierce competition for jobs, housing and services grew worse. As one dramatic example of this competition, a Los Angeles County administrator reported in 1991 that 62 percent of maternity cases in county hospitals involved illegal alien mothers.

As to fertility, public and private efforts to reduce unwanted pregnancies among the poor have been undermined by the abortion debate and the attacks on family planning centers, which Presidents Ronald Reagan and

George Bush at least tacitly supported. The higher pregnancy rate among the poor (of all races; fertility is much more a function of education and economic status than of race) has multiplied the size of the national problem of nurturing and educating poor children to escape the cycle of poverty.

In pursuit of a domestic ideological debate about Chinese population policy, President Bush cut off U.S. support for the U.N. Population Fund and the International Planned Parenthood Foundation. He thus did what he could to postpone third world efforts to address the population problems they themselves recognize and to assure that third world population pressures—and the pressures to migrate to the United States—will continue to rise, offering the prospect of more and bigger "L.A. riots."

Racial and ethnic tensions are the most widespread political phenomena of the post–Cold War era. They are not just U.S. phenomena, and they arise from complex causes; but they feed on joblessness and frustration. The effort to bring minorities (particularly Blacks and Hispanics) into unfettered participation in U.S. society requires good will on all sides and a sustained effort to help the minority poor to master the economic skills of modern society. Even if the country's leadership cannot guarantee everybody the job of his or her choice, it should try to create an environment in which those who are willing and able to work can find work to do.

In this respect, over the past three or four decades, the nation could not have botched the job more thoroughly if it had deliberately set out to start riots. Unemployment, the sense of frustration and hopelessness, and the competition for jobs with people coming from desperate lives in other countries—these were the tinder on which the L.A. riots fed.

The migratory pressures are not finished. They will increase. Figure 1.2 dramatizes the pressures in nearby emigrant-sending regions.[13] It shows, at decade intervals,

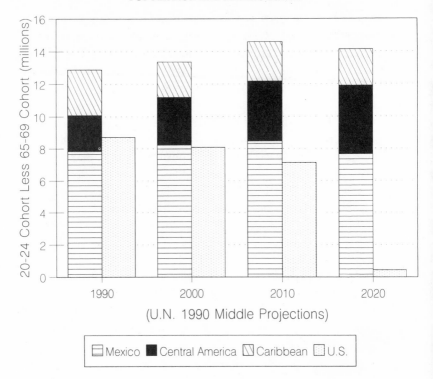

FIGURE 1.2 *Growth of Working-Age Population (entrants less departers)*

the growth of the working-age population, charting the size of the 20-to-24-year-old group entering their working years, minus the 65-to-69-year-olds departing. These projections are not just guesses. The young adults of twenty years hence are already born. The countries of Mesoamerica, bedeviled even now by high unemployment, will have to absorb an expansion of the working-age population as large as the United States did during the 1970s and 1980s when the baby boomers came of age—and those economies in total are 1/17th as large as ours. In this country, during those years, the poor got poorer and the rich got richer. The problems just south of us are likely to be infinitely more intense. If one looks beyond, to South America and the rest of the world, the total numbers are of course far larger.

The immigration problem is not going away. It is growing,

and it will intensify the competition for education, jobs and housing among the nation's young and unskilled.

The government reacted typically to the riots in Los Angeles, appointing a commission to inquire into the behavior of the police and passing emergency legislation to fund some 380,000 jobs, nationwide, for one summer—enough for about 13 percent of the young people who are without jobs.[14] As the Christopher report eventually showed, the police needed investigation, but these are stopgaps rather than solutions.

The nation is preoccupied with finding culprits and it fails to look for fundamental causes. When Congress passed the Immigration Act of 1990 raising immigration quotas, the brief congressional debate reflected no awareness that immigration rates and the tensions in the inner cities might be connected.

Any hope for the inner cities would seem to lie in a complex set of changes involving better education, changes in attitudes both within the inner cities and toward them, and the legitimate prospect of finding jobs. And central to that process is limiting the numbers of those who must escape the cycle of poverty, by holding down immigrant competition and persuading young people to have fewer children, so that educational efforts can be addressed to manageable numbers and job opportunities bear some relationship to the number of job seekers. As a nation, we have not begun that sort of integrated thinking.

The issue is not confined to minorities, or to the cities. Hourly wages, which had been impelled upward by labor shortages and productivity gains for much of our history, peaked in the late 1970s, just as the baby boom generation came on the labor market and as immigration began rising toward its present levels. Wages have not been the same since. The oil crises probably triggered the downward trend, but the correlation between labor supply and its price has certainly reflected the law of supply and demand. Lower wages were no accident. As the rich in this country get richer and the poor get poorer and more numerous, we are coming increasingly to resemble third world societies such as India. Who thought 30 years ago that street sleepers would be a major social problem in 1994?

ENERGY

It used to be easy to believe complacently that the rising prosperity of most Americans during this century—until very recently—was the result of "American know-how" or our particular organizational abilities. It would be more accurate to ascribe that prosperity to our early discovery and exploitation of fossil fuel resources. By the 1970s, our annual use of fossil fuels was about 1.4 times as high as the total primary energy production (the capture of solar energy in plant photosynthesis) in the United States.[15] In other words, we have been living beyond our resources, on fossil energy, just as we have been relying on fossil water in agriculture.

We are now approaching the downslope of the fossil fuel era. Let us take a closer look at U.S. energy sources.

Petroleum

Petroleum will be the first to go. The U.S. Geological Survey (USGS) in 1989 estimated that total remaining petroleum, including known reserves and potential resources still undiscovered, equaled about 16 years' consumption at current rates.[16] The estimate had been driven progressively downward as exploration failed to find petroleum in promising offshore locations.

In 1985, U.S. crude oil production reached a high of 9 million barrels per day, drawing on the new Alaskan fields. By 1993 production stood at only about 6.9 million barrels.[17] Today U.S. reliance on imported oil is about 50 percent of consumption. Two-thirds of the world's estimated petroleum resources are in the Persian Gulf area. How long can we depend on those supplies? How long can we afford them, even if renewed instability in that volatile region does not imperil their availability?

24

Natural Gas

Natural gas resources are somewhat more plentiful than petroleum, but not by much. The USGS estimates total recoverable domestic resources at 671 trillion cubic feet, or enough for about 36 years at the current rate of consumption. (This figure ignores imports, which provide about 3 percent of current consumption.)

When specialists talk of a 36-year supply, beware. There are two deep pitfalls here. First, the projection assumes current consumption levels. If population is rising, either the resource is used faster or the per capita consumption must diminish every year. Second, as oil becomes scarce and the price rises, a shift to gas will occur, accelerating its depletion. (Gas consumption in the 1970s during the oil price shocks was higher than it is now.)

The oil companies know what is happening. Amoco has announced a policy of deemphasizing further exploration in the United States. The four companies that once held the most oil and gas acreage in the United States (Amoco, Exxon, Texaco and Shell) have reduced that acreage by 46 percent as they moved their exploration overseas.[18]

During 1991, by the way, the natural gas industry found new reserves to replace only 85 percent of the natural gas it produced in the lower 48 states, down from 101 percent average replacement in the previous five years.

Coal

We need to move away from fossil fuels not simply because they are being exhausted. They are the principal drivers of climate change, water and soil acidification and the various forms of air pollution.

Coal is our most abundant remaining fossil fuel resource. It is also the dirtiest. If it were not for coal, we could perhaps console ourselves with the thought that environmental damage from fossil fuels will eventually be self-limiting as we run out of them. Not so with coal. About 75 percent of known bituminous coal reserves are in China, the former USSR, and the United States. The United States has proven recoverable reserves of 113 billion metric tons, and that much again in reserves not presently economically recoverable.[19] These reserves represent a supply for a century or two at current levels of consumption (again noting the caveat that consumption levels may change). The prospects for discovering extensive new deposits are remote.

Since the country will become more reliant on coal in the future (barring a remarkably rapid shift to solar and other renewable sources), there are some heavy national investments ahead if the United States is serious about controlling sulfur oxide emissions. At present, some 86 percent of our coal consumption goes into generating electricity, but as recently as 1950 more went into commercial and residential heating than into electricity. We will need to discourage a return to the use of coal in individual furnaces, which by their nature are more polluting than properly designed large thermal electric plants. We will also need to promote a widespread conversion to heat pumps for warming, to use the electricity more efficiently.

If we are not to choke on the added pollution from a greater reliance on coal, the country will need to finance a wholesale conversion of our thermal electric plants to more modern designs. Pilot testing has been carried out on several "clean" systems, notably the IGCC (integrated gasification-combined cycle) process that operated until recently under multiple sponsorship at Cool Water, California. Such new approaches lead to dramatic reductions in pollution and even permit the recovery of the pollutants for commercial use. The principal remaining problem, aside from the cost of the new technology, is that means must still be found to sequester the carbon dioxide emissions to avoid contributing further to global warming.

There are opportunities for the clean use of coal, but only with massive replacement of present generating capacity. Consider this statement from a recent National Acid Precipitation Assessment Program (NAPAP) study: "In the year 2020 . . . sulfur dioxide emissions from utilities were projected to be 5 million tons when a 40-year retirement age was assumed, compared with 19 million tons under a 70-year retirement age assumption."[20] This dramatic difference in air pollution from coal in the two investment scenarios underlines the critical importance of finding the resources to invest in cleaner energy.

The costs do not stop there. The atmosphere is global. None of the other major coal producers—China and the successor states to the USSR—is in a good position to pay a premium for its energy. China in particular, with more than half the Earth's recoverable reserves, is rapidly expanding its use of coal. It is in all countries' interest to encourage China to use the least damaging technology possible, even if the industrial countries must help pay for licensing arrangements or the differential costs of using more benign technologies.

Biomass

People turn to biomass as a solution when they discover that we must move away from fossil fuels. (Biomass fuel is organic matter that can be burned directly or converted to a more convenient gaseous or liquid fuel by distillation or pyrolysis.)

The problem is that biomass must come either from farms or from forests. Recent efforts at biomass conversion (methanol from corn) used more energy than they generated. That problem could be addressed by improving the technology and relying on other sources, such as cornstalks or bagasse from sugarcane, but the dilemma does not end there. Biomass production from agriculture competes with existing uses of the land, and we shall shortly see that agriculture already needs more cropland than it has, for food and fiber production.

Firewood

It sounds almost quaint to speak of firewood, but it is the original form of biomass for conversion to energy. Until

1880, firewood (mostly from local woodlots) provided over half our total energy. It may have been a toilsome resource to extract, but it was close by, and staying warm in the winter did not depend on long gas pipelines or Middle East oil supplies.

Firewood became less and less important, though there was something of a return to it after the second oil crisis. It now provides about 3 percent of total energy consumption. Interestingly enough, the total tonnage of firewood burned is again about the same as in 1880.[21] The difference is that our total energy consumption has gone up 17-fold.

Environmentalists at first looked on the return to firewood as somehow desirable. Indeed, if the woodlots are well maintained and replanted, they harvest energy production from current photosynthesis and do not run down the resource. They therefore do not add to the problem of carbon dioxide in the atmosphere. However, the enthusiasm for wood burning is fading. It turned out that wood fires (particularly in the efficient airtight stoves popular in the 1970s) themselves are a source of air pollution. The little resort town of Telluride, Colorado, achieved a certain fame in this regard. Controlled by environmental activists, and located in a box canyon, it quickly discovered that its charming wood fires were generating dense smog. The town government enacted ordinances requiring that smoke detectors be installed in all chimney flues and regulating how often one could have a wood fire. Other towns, in one way or the other, have had to follow suit. There are environmental limits to the use of wood as a household fuel.

Over time, there is a more ominous consequence of the shift to firewood. It is a singularly vulnerable resource. If we may offer anecdotal evidence on a matter where hard data are notoriously weak, let us cite what happened in the Appalachians west of Washington, D.C., in the 1970s, when oil became expensive and wood fashionable. The whine of chain saws reached a crescendo in the autumn, as countrymen laid in their winter wood supplies and cut for the expanded suburban market. An observer familiar with the area could see the spines of the ridges as the woodlands were thinned out. In the West, and particularly in the National Forests, firewood poaching is a serious problem. If (or rather, when) there is another fuel crisis, illegal wood gathering will probably become a critical threat to watersheds and standing timber in many areas. It is politically difficult for the U.S. Forest Service to take stern action against such seemingly harmless activity by people who need the firewood.

For reasons that will become clear later in this chapter, the timber statistics lag behind the reality and may actually be falsified. The impending pressures on fossil fuels may in fact create a serious threat to our forests.

Nuclear Energy

Nuclear energy offers a devil's choice. It doesn't generate the sorts of pollution that fossil fuels do. However, the dangers are all too obvious and have been well publicized by Three Mile Island, Chernobyl, and the waste management problems already mentioned. Moreover, uranium supplies, like fossil fuels, are finite. Nuclear energy is itself no more than a transitional fuel unless one turns to plutonium or the breeder reactor, both of which intensify all the problems of "conventional" nuclear energy: radiation accidents, nuclear proliferation, theft and the possible conversion to weapons by any reasonably sophisticated technical organization.

We didn't need to have this dilemma. If the U.S. population were still what it was during World War II, as Paul and Anne Ehrlich point out, the United States, even without cutting its consumption habits, could meet its energy appetite "without burning one drop of imported oil or one ounce of coal."[22] (In fairness, be it said that in that case we would still be heading toward an energy crisis, albeit at a slower pace, since consumption goes on and resources are finite.)

New Technologies

The way out of the energy crisis probably lies in solar, wind, geothermal and perhaps other new and exotic technologies, along with such innovations as the introduction of fuel cells and pure hydrogen as a fuel. There may also be hope for nuclear fusion, if scientists ever learn to make it generate more energy than it consumes. We shouldn't count on it, or forget that fission energy was once promised as a clean and inexhaustible source. What will we learn about the side effects of fusion?

The shift to renewable sources is technically feasible. (A NASA study once pointed out that, theoretically, we could meet U.S. energy needs with wind power alone.)[23] From what we presently know about those technologies, they are relatively benign, environmentally.

The problem is to get on with it. The major roadblock right now is government policy. As long as oil gushes out of the ground in the Persian Gulf region, it will be cheaper than developing new technologies—assuming that we can afford the foreign exchange to buy it, that the Middle Eastern countries do not exploit their monopoly position, and that political instability does not endanger the supply. This price differential has discouraged companies from moving more aggressively into the new technologies. The government could close the price gap with sufficient taxes on fossil and nuclear fuels. Such taxes would not necessarily be a distortion of the market. The energy companies are now having a free ride. They and ultimately the users should be taxed for the immediate environmental costs of our reliance on these fuels, and perhaps for the military costs of attempting to assure a stable supply of oil from abroad. Regrettably, no imaginable tax will pay for the societal costs of climate change generated by fossil fuels, or probably the cleanup costs and continuing risks from the nuclear power industry.

The center of the problem is money. All in all, it appears that we will be paying a very stiff price for our gradual emergence from the fossil fuel era. The conversion promises to be one of the most expensive structural changes that humankind has yet undertaken.

Population enters the situation in two ways. First, the total size of the population (returning to the formula *Impact* = *Population* × *Consumption Levels* × *Technology*) will determine just how much energy capacity must be built. Second, there is a competition for available capital between this new investment and the social expenditures necessary to deal with our urban problems and to provide for (and attempt to control) the large and growing population of unskilled people outside our economic mainstream.[24] Alienation imposes high costs, including lost creativity and labor and the expense of dealing with crime, drugs, vandalism and welfare dependency.

Again, we encounter an interlocking connection between the costs of a large population per se and the incremental costs imposed by the high fertility and immigration rates that lead to a large population.

FORESTS

It is fashionable to berate the Brazilians for allowing the destruction of their rainforests, but as a pair of NASA photographs recently dramatized,[25] the United States is cutting down its remaining old-growth forests much more thoroughly.

The old coniferous forests of the Northwest are disappearing. The saddest part is that we are letting it happen in our National Forests. The demand for sawtimber, simply put, has proven politically irresistible. Western senators have turned into bare-knuckled advocates for excessive forest exploitation. Responding to the pressure, the Forest Service now issues harvest quotas to its Regional Foresters from Washington, D.C., rather than following the earlier practice of determining locally the sustainable cut on the basis of what the forests could bear. This change—and the increasing pressures to get out the cut at the expense of

31

biological diversity—led to an unprecedented rebellion within the Forest Service. In 1989, a group of employees created AFSEEE (Association of Forest Service Employees for Environmental Ethics) to protest the mismanagement of our National Forests. Shortly thereafter, all ten western regional forest supervisors sent memoranda to Forest Service Chief F. Dale Robertson protesting that current policies violated their responsibility for land stewardship under the multiple-use philosophy decreed by the National Forest Management Act of 1976.[26]

The Forest Service management responded with soft words. It instituted a "New Perspectives" campaign with the publicized adoption of "Ecosystem Management"— and it began to transfer or force out those who complained, including at least one Regional Forester. Citizen action was circumvented by eliminating the provision for public appeals of Forest Service "decision notices" announcing harvesting plans. The cut goes on.

Rising demand, driven by population growth, may be leading us onto a very serious path of self-delusion. It is one thing to overcut. It is more serious when data are doctored to hide the overcut. There have been several disturbing indications recently that this is happening. In the spring of 1992, a Forest Service stand examiner testified under oath before a hearing of the House Interior Appropriations Subcommittee that the Forest Service keeps two sets of data on standing timber, and that the "FORPLAN" figures, on which cutting plans and congressional presentations are based, overstated standing timber in the Kootenai National Forest by 36 percent and ignored 75 percent of the clearcuts. He went on to say that the classification system systematically overstates standing timber.[27] He documented his charges with aerial photographs.

A conservation group created after that testimony, the Inventory Inquiry Project, systematically compared the two Forest Service inventories for the Kootenai and came up with even worse figures. The U.S. Fish and Wildlife Service official responsible for grizzly bear habitat in the Kootenai came to similar conclusions in a very forceful memorandum.[28]

Perhaps most telling, the House Committee on Interior and Insular Affairs staff assembled a growing number of accounts of how the Forest Service and the BLM (Bureau of Land Management, Interior Department) "overestimated timber inventories and overstated reforestation success" in the Northwest and California. While the staff did not attempt to quantify the results, the collection of reports on each forest is somber reading.[29]

Falsification of data is a disturbing development. Denial is hardly the way to a cure. This precedent is an ominous one for our entire statistical system.

What is driving this process is not just greed, though there is plenty of that in the industry. A dying industry generates serious local unemployment problems. Denial, however, simply defers the problem and leaves a devastated ecology when the forests do run out.

Contrary to the popular impression, our forest problems do not stem from our exports. True, we were net importers until about 1962. With growing world demand we have become exporters, but exports still represent less than 5 percent of our total production of roundwood. Domestic demand is the problem. And that demand is population-driven. From 1950 until the late 1980s, population and domestic wood consumption both rose about two-thirds.[30] In other words, the threat to our forests is a result of the effort to keep up with population growth.

As to forest resources and population, the official numbers tell a revealing story, optimistic though they may be.

From 1952 until 1987, the figures for total standing timber rose by 24 percent.[31] The official estimate of standing stock in the West declined 10 percent in the period. The growth was in Southeastern pine plantations—a reflection of the same trend toward monoculture that makes our agriculture vulnerable—and in unmanaged Northeastern hardwood forests. (Pastures that once fed work horses before the advent of the tractor are still reverting to woodland.) So far so good. The hitch is that our total population in that period rose by 57 percent, so the per capita timber stand went down 21 percent—even if the data are not cooked.

Over-harvesting is not the only threat to our forests. The industrial age itself threatens them, in the form of pollution, acid rain and the prospect of rapid global warming. The extent and causes of forest damage are too contentious and complex a subject for treatment in a general overview. The range of opinion is best shown in the difference between the official German view of damage to their forests and the conclusions of NAPAP, the most extensive U.S. study. In 1985, the Germans estimated that 52 percent of their forests had been damaged by acid rain. The 1992 NAPAP study, by contrast, concluded that the United States had suffered "no widespread forest or crop damage" from acid rain other than to sugar maples in some areas and to high-altitude spruce and pines.[32] This is an optimistic assessment, but other studies suggest that some combination of acidity, pollutants (particularly tropospheric ozone) and specific soil deficiencies combine to damage forests.

Intuitively, one would assume that climate warming will harm or at least change forests, particularly if conditions get drier. Although little research exists to support a more concrete prediction, at least one intriguing theory has been proposed, based on the rate at which certain tree species are known to have "migrated" northward to cooler climes at the beginning of the current warming cycle. The theory suggests that, if global warming continues as the major models predict, the speed of warming will exceed the speed at which the forests can move northward, wiping out most of certain species such as beech.[33]

At the most sanguine, the conclusion is that U.S. forests are potentially threatened by the present pattern of industrial growth and economic activity, which in turn reflects the size and growth of the population to be served.

AGRICULTURE

Compared with most of the world, the United States is well endowed with agricultural land. We have 0.75 hectares of arable land per person, compared with 0.12 hectares for the United Kingdom or 0.08 hectares for China. Nevertheless, we are entering a technological trap because, like the other advanced countries, we have moved to high-yield monocultures dependent on several unreliable inputs: fertilizers, which are becoming less and less effective; groundwater pumping, at a rate 25 percent faster than aquifers are being recharged;[34] the continuing development of crop varieties that require the additional fertilizer and water; fossil fuels to run tractors and make fertilizer—as the petroleum era draws to a close; and pesticides, which over the years lose potency as pesticide-resistant pests evolve.

The trap is this: we have adopted these technologies to meet the rising demand of a growing population, but the technologies are not sustainable over the long term, and they are a major source of environmental damage.

The rise in agricultural yields since 1950, in the United States and most of the world, historically is unparalleled. More than half of U.S. agricultural production today is dependent on the new inputs described above.[35] A convenient measure is to compare U.S. production of cereals in 1948–1950, when the technologies were just coming into widespread use, with present production. Today we are producing 2.2 times as much tonnage on 79 percent of the earlier acreage. That is a remarkable gain in yield of 2.5 percent per year over a 40-year period. Nothing like that has occurred before, anywhere.

The question is: Can we keep it up? Agricultural technologies are becoming more expensive, or less effective, or running into absolute limits.

We have used technological props to keep ahead of demand, but consider what they do to the environment: accelerated soil erosion resulting from monocultures and the associated heavy equipment; the degrading of wetlands and tidal areas where fish breed, due to fertilizer runoff and pesticide poisoning; threats to our own health from the poisoning of groundwater supplies; the accelerated release of methane and of nitrous oxides that contribute to climate warming, acid precipitation and ozone depletion.

With massive investment, subsidies to the agricultural sector that run about $12 billion per year,[36] and serious damage to the environment, what have we really achieved?

Erosion

The Department of Agriculture's estimate of annual U.S. cropland erosion is 3 billion tons.[37] That works out to about 18 tons per hectare, annually. Some of our most fertile and deep soils (such as in Iowa or eastern Washington State) have lost about half their topsoil in the century or so they have been cultivated. In less fortunate areas, soils are now too thin to accommodate root growth. Topsoil loss reduces production and requires heavier fertilization. The rate of decline is highly dependent on local conditions, but the key point is that we are literally losing rather than gaining ground, and the effect on future agricultural production is necessarily negative.

Fertilizers

The effectiveness of fertilizers is on the decline. The Worldwatch Institute reports, for example, that in the corn belt an additional ton of fertilizer now produces only one-quarter as much corn as it did in the 1960s.[38] Even if it were not for that inconvenient problem, we need to limit the use of nitrates and phosphates for environmental reasons. The discovery in 1913 of a way to extract nitrogen from the atmosphere, together with the exploitation of the great Florida phosphate deposits, has led to the introduction of nitrogen and phosphorus compounds into the environment at a rate rivaling or surpassing natural releases. These compounds are poisoning our groundwater, wiping out coastal fisheries (oyster harvests in the Chesapeake Bay have declined about 80 percent in this century)[39] and perhaps generating the problems in our oceans that will be described later.

Phosphate fertilizer use may in some degree be self-limiting, since the higher-grade U.S. deposits are being exhausted. Future supplies will probably cost more and may have to be imported.[40]

Irrigation

In the future, the prospects are for less water for irrigation. Urban demand and the need to protect wetlands threaten the cheap, subsidized irrigation supplies in California, our largest agricultural producer. Moreover, the groundwater aquifers are subsiding in areas where agriculture has become critically dependent on them. The Ogallala Aquifer in the plains states is the largest and most important example. Some experts estimate that it may be entirely depleted within the next 25 years.[41] As the water table subsides, the cost of pumping the water rises. As energy costs rise, the cost of pumping water will rise even faster. The prospect, already a reality in some areas, is for a reversion to lower-yield dry land agriculture or, on fragile soils, to rangeland.

Pesticides

Pesticide applications have increased around 33-fold since World War II (the range of estimates is enormous). Nevertheless, the loss of potential harvests to pests keeps rising. Losses from insect pests alone are estimated to have doubled from 7 to 13 percent in that period. In the case of one major crop, continuous monoculture cultivation of corn, pesticide applications have risen 1,000-fold, but losses to insects have risen 4-fold.[42]

The pests can absorb enormous losses from pesticides without being wiped out. Farmers here and abroad have been engaged in a gigantic, uncontrolled and unplanned experiment, learning what new and ever more ferocious pests will evolve in the cauldron of accelerated environmental change as they adapt to handle new pesticides. Having won an early round, thanks to the explosion of pesticide technology in the 1950s and 1960s, farmers are now on the defensive. One expert reports that "447 species of insects, ticks, and mites are now resistant to some or all pesticides."[43] Another estimate put the number of resistant agricultural arthropod pests at 260 species as of 1980.[44] Even more alarming is the fact that at least one pest has developed resistance to a strain of biopesticide, *Bacillus thuringiensis*, that had been heralded as a promising new "natural" control.[45]

These ephemeral gains in agricultural productivity have other costs as well. Pesticides work their way into streams, rainwater and groundwater, where they threaten birds and wildlife, beneficial insects such as bees, and human health. In health terms alone, a National Academy of Sciences report suggested that as many as 1.46 million cases of human cancer may result from exposure to pesticide residues. Since the banning of DDT a generation ago, a national tug-of-war has raged over the use of various pesticides.[46] For our purposes, the important point is that pesticides are becoming less and less effective; they remain thoroughly dangerous, and there is no reason to expect that they will continue to boost agricultural yields as they did for 30 or 40 years.

Nevertheless, we are hooked on pesticides because, in modern monocultures, the pests would take over if we ceased their application.

To grapple with these problems, crop improvement efforts in coming decades may need to focus on pest resistance rather than crop responses to fertilizers.

The lesson is that you don't go very far on a treadmill.

There are ways to get off the treadmill: a reversion to crop rotation to deprive the pests periodically of their habitat; the use of different varieties, not just the highest-yielding ones, to reduce the vulnerability of crops to epidemics; the return to windbreaks and shelterbelts to help hold the soil in place, particularly where farmers must return to dry land farming. (We learned about shelterbelts after the Dust Bowl and then abandoned them for boundary-to-boundary fields for greater production.) We could practice organic farming, reduced tillage and harvesting practices that leave more organic material in the soil. These practices reduce the dependence on artificial nitrogen fertilizer, arrest erosion and counteract the compaction of the soil under heavy agricultural machinery.

The nation's farmers have already embraced the last of these approaches. "Conservation farming," with reduced tillage and the retention of crop residues, was still a curiosity in 1980. It is now used on more than one-quarter of our cropland.[47] This shift may be responsible for one of the healthier recent trends: commercial fertilizer use, which peaked in 1980, has dropped by more than 15 percent. Crop production has been fluctuating since then, but overall it is up, rather than down.[48] This record offers hope that more benign agricultural practices may be practicable.

The problem is that most of those approaches will probably mean smaller yields. They can be put in effect without imperiling our diets or our exports only if demand—and therefore population—can be held constant or reduced. Genetic engineering has not yet resulted in any real breakthrough that would increase yields dramatically, and at present no techniques exist to maintain the sort of growth we have enjoyed since the 1950s.

We could adopt the reforms described above without starving Americans, at least at this stage. We could phase out our heavy consumption of meat and rely increasingly on grains and vegetables. For a while, the shift would be dietetically good for us. When we have used up that slack, however, the question arises: "What next?" With current demographic trends carrying us toward millions and millions more people in the next century, with current practices damaging our soils, with an uncertain energy future, with the prospect that irrigation will necessarily decline, with the decreasing effectiveness of pesticides and with the uncertainties associated with acid precipitation and climate change, the possibility of real hunger may not seem so remote two or three generations hence.

The incurable optimist says "If we are efficient we can, like Japan and the newly industrializing countries, import food and finance it with exports." But where would we import the food from, in a world where we have been the residual food exporter? (In 1990, we supplied about two-thirds of the corn and soybeans entering world trade, and almost one-third of the wheat.)[49] In fact, the inability of the United States to export food would result in starvation in some countries most dependent on our food exports.

In the face of serious unresolved uncertainties concerning the progress of agricultural production, we would be well advised to control our demand—and that means limiting our population size, while we still have time.

BIODIVERSITY

The current or threatened elimination of familiar species stirs sympathy that is politically very potent. Our government, responding to public feelings, has expended considerable effort on protecting whales, dolphins enmeshed in tuna nets, various designated endangered species and migratory songbirds.

Our national policies, understandably, address the things we notice. Our laws protect creatures we can see and identify with—mammals and birds, mostly—but not those that shape our environment. The Endangered Species Act focuses on the "higher" taxa. There are 61 species of mammals listed, 85 of birds, 87 of fishes, 81 of all invertebrates, 240 of plants, but no microbes or simple plants. The list reflects a very simplistic view of biodiversity. Opinion leaders and policy makers seem to be thoroughly confused. A furious debate rages over the snail darter and the spotted owl, while we ignore organisms that are fundamental to our survival.

We humans tend to think of ourselves as the principal inhabitants of the Earth. Yet there are very few of us—or of all vertebrates taken together—compared to the insect tribe. As one entomologist wryly remarked: "Bugs are not going to inherit the Earth. They own it now. So we might as well make our peace with the landlord." Another scientist, by way of corroboration, estimated that in the Brazilian Amazon basin the social insects alone outweigh—literally—the mammal population by a ratio of 7 to 1.[50] And each of those insects is an organism struggling to perpetuate itself.

As to microbes, they outnumber us by literally billions to one. And it is, particularly, the microbes that have shaped and maintain the environment, for better or worse. We are quite capable of crippling the Earth's regenerative capacity without noticing it, because we cannot readily see the co-inhabitants that we are endangering.

The role of "lower" orders is not limited to providing humans with medicines such as penicillin. Their function can be as obvious as pollination: most of the flowering plants and trees (angiosperms) depend for survival on bees and other insects.

The role can be more mysterious and even more fundamental. Witness this ominous speculation, from a Presidential Acid Rain Review Committee, appointed by (of all people) President Reagan:

> We as a committee are especially concerned about possible deleterious effects of a sustained increase in the acidity of unmanaged soils. Its microorganism population is particularly sensitive to a change in acidity. But it is just this bottom part of the biological cycle that is responsible for the recycling of nitrogen and carbon in the food chain. The proper functioning of the denitrifying microbes is a fundamental requirement upon which the entire biosphere depends. The evidence that increased acidity is perturbing populations of microorganisms is scanty, but the prospect of such an occurrence is grave.[51]

One has to read that statement twice to realize how fundamentally important it is. The "entire biosphere" includes all of us.

So far, fortunately, ongoing acid precipitation studies do not suggest that the threat is proximate. But we still lack critical evidence, in part because NAPAP, which produced the principal study on acid rain, failed to pursue the long-term effects of acid precipitation on soils and forest ecosystems.[52]

In short, here at the close of the twentieth century and amid a shift of world attention to environmental issues, we fail to take notice of the most numerous and fundamental components of the animal kingdom, and we simply do not yet understand the functioning of the ecosystems that support them and us. Even at the time of our apparent triumph, humankind wields the partial power to destroy but not the power to sustain. The record so far suggests that we are pretty bad managers. The human tribe is connected with the other tribes of the Earth in a far more complex relationship than we had imagined.

There are mysterious die offs of species of frogs and salamanders that had been around for 200 million years and survived the Cretaceous extinctions. A mysterious decline of mushrooms and fungi in Europe may further stress host trees already suffering from acid rain, since the trees and the fungi are symbiotic.[53]

There are diebacks of coral reefs, of dolphins off our coast and of European harbor seals. The deadly "red tides" kill fish farther north along our Atlantic coast than before. Amnesic shellfish poisoning has turned up in the Gulf of St. Lawrence, caused by diatoms that heretofore had been considered nontoxic, while a potentially lethal paralytic toxin has appeared for the first time in Alaskan shellfish. There is "brown slime" in the Adriatic, and the "brown tide" has wiped out the scallop industry off Long Island.[54] The precise cause of this burst of activity in the oceans is not known, but it is thought to be associated with the pumping of nutrients (especially nitrogen and phosphorus) into coastal waters from agricultural and sewage runoff.[55]

Many signals suggest that the explosion of human activity is having profound and deleterious effects on ecological systems, but human knowledge is not yet up to comprehending just what the causes and ramifications may be. The second of two joint statements by the National Academy of Sciences and the Royal Society of London (following the one on population already cited) warned of the threat posed by the loss of biological diversity and called for the creation, worldwide and particularly in tropical countries, of institutes to promote the preservation and wise use of habitats and species.[56]

There is a bitter irony in all this. Human activity is killing off species that enrich our lives or that may be of use to us, and promoting the evolution of species that harm us. Scholars worry that we are creating a manmade environment; in reality we are simply ruining the existing environment, to our own detriment and that of other species.

The key factor is habitat destruction. Wherever we destroy their habitat, we eliminate species, including sometimes those that—whether we have yet learned it or not —can be of benefit to us or perhaps even essential to our survival. By and large, the species on the Endangered Species List got there because we destroyed their habitat.

On the other hand, we create other kinds of habitat— such as giant cornfields and crowded slums—and other species learn to thrive in them, usually by preying on us or on the things that we seek to raise. The microbes and insects can take enormous losses, so long as they have a viable environment. The effort to control them with antibiotics or chemicals means that, in an otherwise hospitable environment, survival favors the strains that are resistant to that particular toxin. Our efforts to exterminate them simply lead to rapid evolutionary improvements that make them more resilient.

In discussing agriculture, we have cited some examples of human promotion of various forms of unwanted biodiversity. Let us cite some others.

Cholera reappeared in 1991 in Peru, after a lapse of many years. It thrived on the windborne dust of fecal matter blowing around the shanty cities that have sprung up around Lima, themselves the product of runaway population growth in the hinterland. The cholera didn't stay there. It has spread northward as far as Mexico, killing over 6,000 people in Latin America since its initial reappearance.[57] There was a scare when it appeared in Los Angeles, transported by an airline passenger. Modern transportation makes neighbors of us all.

A number of viral diseases have developed, mutated and spread because of the expansion of human activities and the worldwide movement of people and organic materials. The influenza "A" virus breeds and mutates in Chinese ducks and pigs, which spread it to humans (they live very close together in China), who in turn pass it on through travel and commerce to the rest of the world. The deadly Ebola virus reached the United States in laboratory monkeys from the Philippines. The Argentine virus that causes hemorrhagic fever spread when the pampas were cleared for corn cultivation, which led to the proliferation of the field mouse that harbors the virus.[58]

Antibiotics, now almost universally used in animal feed in the United States, apparently led to the development of drug-resistant salmonella in the animals, which, when eaten by humans, cause severe intestinal ailments.[59]

After generations of decline, tuberculosis is on the rise, and a new drug-resistant strain—presumably created by the selection process described above—has arisen. By 1991 the new strain was reported in 36 states and had resulted in at least 13 deaths in the New York prison system alone.[60] Tuberculosis is a disease of crowded slums. Its resurgence, coupled with its new drug resistance, has led the World Health Organization to declare it a "global health emergency," predicting that it will kill 30 million people worldwide in the next decade.[61]

People in the United States are dying from the newly discovered hantavirus.

Science magazine described the emergence of viral and bacterial resistance to antibiotics as a "crisis," saying:

Those who believed a plague could not happen in this century have already seen the beginning of one in the

AIDS crisis, but the drug-resistant strains in this issue, which can be transmitted by casual contact in movie theaters, hospitals and shopping centers, are likely to be even more terrifying.[62]

In medicine, as in agriculture, we are watching what the *Science* editorial called "a subterranean war." Microorganisms are responding to and being transformed by the poisons and antibiotics that have been unleashed upon them for the past two generations. Humankind is being subjected, in a sense, to a counterattack in a war that we thought we had won. (The U.S. Surgeon General in 1969 declared that the war against infectious disease was effectively finished.)

This sudden and sobering turn of events should purge us of the hubris that has grown with the scientific and technological successes of recent decades. We had thought we were masters of the Earth, when in fact we have been agents of disruption, and the disruption has been tolerable only because—until these explosive last few decades—the Earth's ecosystems had the capacity to absorb and buffer most of the damage. We are past that point.

We saw ourselves as dominant, and invincible, when in fact we are only one small part of the system. We are vulnerable to the natural consequences of the disruption we have generated, as the pathogens and microorganisms adjust to the fury of our recent attack.

This changed appreciation of humans' relationship to the rest of nature should profoundly influence our view of the human tendency to appropriate large parts of the system for our own use. Few people would want science to abandon the "subterranean war" against pathogens, but a fundamental change of strategy may be needed. We aren't going to overwhelm the pathogens with chemical warfare, so we may need all the help we can get from other organisms that have developed defenses against them or that prey on them. For example, we may need to protect the monkeys that carry the Ebola virus, to learn how they have adjusted

45

biologically to live with a virus that is deadly to humans. The very complexity of nature may be our best ally in this undeclared war.

The point here is that we have an interest, not just in protecting certain species that we know we may need, but in preserving the complexity of the biosystem itself, because we don't know what the next threat will be or what genetic characteristics, hidden somewhere in nature, may help to deal with it. We should look at the rest of the life forms in the biosphere as fellow travelers on the Earth and as maintainers of the environment. We must begin to take a less cavalier view of human activities that disturb ecological systems.

Not all the ills described in this chapter are the result of population growth. (The emergence of AIDS and the proliferation of Asian flu, for example, more likely have their roots in modern mores and communications, which provided the pathogens with opportunities to move into new and hospitable environments.) Most of the disturbances, however, have been driven by population growth: the sludge and toxic wastes, the hydrocarbons and agricultural runoff that are fouling our coastal waters; the use and misuse of fossil fuel; the destruction of our forests; the ignorant proliferation of chemicals; the advent of intensive agriculture; the overcrowding of our cities that led to the reappearance of cholera in Peru and promotes the spread of diseases of crowding such as tuberculosis in the United States. We ourselves suffer when pampas are replaced by grain fields, or virgin forests with tree farms, or wetlands with superhighways and shopping malls. We ourselves are threatened when our pollution threatens forests or, finally, the denitrifying microbes described in the 1983 report of the Presidential Committee.

Since these changes are driven by total demand and therefore in part by population growth, we will reduce the threats to the ecosystem by stopping or reversing further growth.

Quite practically, we had better save a system that, eventually, may save us from inadvertent self-destruction as we tinker with a planet we do not fully understand.

Beyond that, usefulness to the human tribe is not necessarily the only standard we should apply when we consider the human role in promoting the extinction of some species and the proliferation of others. Reasonable modesty and a sense of prudence both suggest that we should leave a substantial fraction of nature unengineered. Philosophically, the preservation of the complexity of the global ecosystem into which we were born would seem far preferable to a world barren of all life but our own artifacts. The Endangered Species Act and the drive to create designated Wilderness Areas are evidence of the strength of this generous impulse among Americans.

After this century of unprecedented and accelerating disturbance, we need to make a conscious decision to preserve a considerable part of the biosphere as free as possible from human interference. That decision inevitably will constrict the area and resources that we can manipulate, as well as our freedom to continue dumping pollutants into the air and water. Thus the population factor arises again. Denying ourselves those options will limit the total resources available to humans and the freedom to dispose of wastes. If we are interested in preserving the owl or the whale—or ourselves—will conservation and technology alone allow humankind to get by on the reduced resources? Or must we address P—population—the fundamental driver in the $I = PCT$ formula?

THE TORN WEB

Taken together, what does all this evidence, from sewage sludge to endangered species, suggest?

There are two conflicting visions of where we stand as a nation. One sees us simply as being at an indefinite point on an upward curve, with growth in all directions lying before us. The other sees us at a point just beyond the peak of such a period, facing the limitations that unrestrained growth has itself generated. Humankind has a very short attention span, and it would be comfortable to believe that a brief spurt of growth unparalleled in history could be maintained indefinitely, but the evidence summarized in this chapter makes a compelling case for the second viewpoint. Difficult though their task is, scientists are telling the nation that the free ride is close to being over.

The industrial era, the accompanying transformation of agriculture and the pattern of life that our society has built on the temporary foundation of fossil energy have skewed and threatened the underpinnings of our lives, from the livability of our cities to the life support systems around us.

In some respects, such as the use of certain chemicals or the appropriation of wilderness to human use, we may simply have to stop doing certain things. In other areas, such as toxic and nuclear waste cleanup, we face horrendous bills to undo the damage our society has already done, and higher prices to transform, recycle or safely dispose of the toxins that we have heretofore simply dumped on the environment. In still other spheres, such as agriculture, we may need to unlearn new practices and relearn those we have abandoned, at considerable potential loss of production. In the case of energy, we face both the enormous capital costs of the shift to sustainable sources and the prospect that energy will be more expensive in that new era than it has been during the halcyon years when it simply gushed out of holes in the ground.

Behavior that is socially acceptable when there is little pressure on the land becomes unacceptable when the pressure rises. There is a tradeoff between individual freedom and social responsibility, and freedom is circumscribed as the pressures increase. To give a few examples: Not all the old-growth stands in the Northwest are on public land. Many of the old stands on private lands may need to be protected, but their owners will see such action as taking their property. In the Southeastern woodlands, the forest is mostly private. Preservation of biological diversity urgently demands that some mixed stands be preserved or reinstated among the endless pine tree farms, particularly along the stream and river bottoms. The same is true of Western ranch lands. In the high plains, land that reverted to range after the Dust Bowl is being converted back to cropping, thanks to our tax and agricultural subsidy policies, setting the scene for another Dust Bowl. In all these cases, the public interest comes in conflict with tenaciously held private interests and with the thoroughly American mindset that one has a right to do what one pleases with one's own land.

We have recently gone through the most sudden and drastic alteration of the human condition in history, and the correction of its excesses will require profound adjustments and costs. Because the United States carried the industrial revolution so far, we will be paying a major share of that cost.

In a sense, the bill has come due. In case after case, the growth of economic activity and its concomitant pollution—which in sheer physical terms often dwarfs the economic product—has overwhelmed the absorptive capacity of the biosphere. We must now begin not only to pay the cleanup costs but to assess and hold ourselves accountable for the true costs of that activity. We can no longer allow society to "externalize" the cost of our waste by simply throwing it away.

The United States is already beginning to change its habits to address these problems, even though we still perceive them dimly and in fragmented fashion. The 1970s wave of environmental legislation and the recent enthusiasm for recycling are evidence of that spirit. We should be of good heart. Stabilization is not the end of the world. Most nations in history have necessarily lived within tight resource constraints. After all, they didn't have an empty continent in which to shape an ethics of unlimited space and resources.

The element to be added to the national will to do something about these problems is, of course, population. It is critical that we as a nation realize that an expansionist view

49

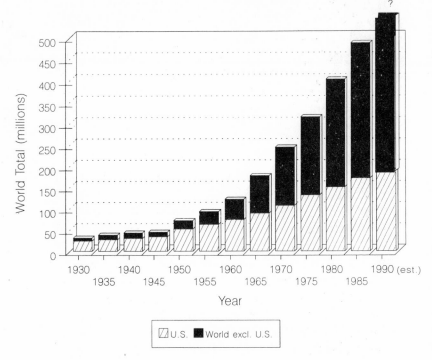

Source: *U.N. Statistical Yearbook*, various years; and *Statistical Abstract of the U.S.*, 1992.

FIGURE 1.3 *Motor Vehicles (autos and commercial)*

of population, given the inevitable limits of future economic growth, is a prescription for increasing misery, since it means that consumption per capita must keep declining.

LESSONS FROM THE AUTOMOBILE

These abstractions can be set in perspective by looking at a single phenomenon: the internal combustion motor vehicle. This is not simply an arbitrary case study. The automobile is connected with most of the issues we have described. Indeed, for a machine that hardly predates this century, it occupies a remarkable role in our economic and social world. To get an idea of the growth of U.S. and total world automobile numbers since 1930, see figure 1.3.[63]

The automobile (the generic term is used here to cover commercial vehicles as well as private cars) has revolutionized our lives in America. We can go more places and see more things, eat a wider variety of foods at any season, buy more different things than ever before and conveniently carry them home. Physical movement has become simplified as never before.

In the process, the automobile has done a remarkable amount of damage. As a part of the environment, the automobile was insignificant until well into the century. Because of the recent explosion of numbers, it is now the principal source of urban air pollution and, along with thermal electricity generation, the principal contributor to both acid precipitation and the greenhouse effect. It is the least controllable source of ozone depletion and rising ultraviolet radiation, since the chlorofluorocarbons (CFCs) in automobile air conditioners are not usually recovered when the cars crash, age, or are abandoned.

Indirectly, the automobile has contributed to environmental problems in other ways as well. It permitted middle-class flight to the suburbs, thereby intensifying the isolation of the poor in the urban ghettoes and the financial crises of the cities. The infrastructure that supports the automobile—from the interstate highways to the gas-station tanks leaking into groundwater supplies—generates environmental damage of its own. The automobile has contributed to the solid waste problem simply because it is so easy to buy and carry home more merchandise, and then throw it away. Vehicle carcasses litter the landscape or occupy valuable landfills. The automobile has damaged fragile terrain and its plants and animals, as vacationers spread out over more of the land and off-road vehicles do what they were designed to do.

The automobile is profoundly inefficient. A person, walking, uses perhaps two or three times as much energy as when at rest. Put him or her in a car, and less than 2 percent of the expended energy moves the driver, while another 13 percent or so moves the vehicle, and the rest is discharged as pollution and heat.[64] Can we continue to endure such inefficiencies as the petroleum era draws to a close?

There are things to be learned from figure 1.3 other than sheer numbers. For example, this graph should permanently nail the lid on the myth of "X years of consumption at the present rates." "Present rates" are not static; they are growing rapidly. Total worldwide reserves and estimated resources of petroleum (most of it in the Persian Gulf states) are equal to about 69 years' worth, at current consumption rates.[65] But given the extraordinary growth rate of world motor vehicle fleets (5.5 percent annually in recent years), that supply looks to be closer to 30 years' worth. Clearly, something has to give.

Until 1965, most of the world's automobiles were in the United States. Since then, the rest of the world has been catching up, but it still has a long way to go. In the United States, there is now about one vehicle per person of driving age (17 and over). Presumably, we are about saturated, and future growth of the U.S. auto fleet will be limited by the growth of the adult population. For the rest of the world, taken together, the ratio is still about 1 to 8.

The common folk of the world seem to have been thoroughly sold on the "American way of life," including the automobile. Yet, as we have seen, they are not going to get there, for both environmental and resource reasons. That is not, however, a message that politicians will be happy to carry to them. There have been a few recent tentative successes (CFCs; nitrogen and sulfur oxides) in addressing global environmental issues through international cooperation. If advances are to continue, and not be brought to a halt by competition for Middle Eastern oil and political timidity, the United States will be under intense pressure to reduce the margin by which it is favored in using fossil fuels and generating pollution. For the sake of the Earth, it can no longer afford to stay in the "lead" in these areas.

To those with a short perspective, the solution is simple: use natural gas. All this does, though, is defer the transition by a few decades, particularly since world resources, now estimated at 139 years' *current consumption* worldwide, is also facing increasing demand and will be exhausted even faster as it replaces oil. (The U.S. figure, as we have seen, is about a 36-year supply.)

The worst possible scenario is this: the nations scramble for the remaining oil supplies without cooperating in an orderly energy transition, thus shortening the transition and making it much more disruptive and costly. The international effort to control emissions collapses. Those who have it, burn it. In particular, those who have coal (China, the United States, Russia) turn to it without putting the best available technology into controlling the pollution.

From time to time in this chapter, mention has been made of the extraordinarily costly catch-up the nation must go through to correct the "externalities"—the pollution and resource destruction—involved in our present forms of economic behavior. Add to that the costs of converting to renewable energy sources. And now add the capital costs of transforming a society that has been built around the automobile. The whole layout of the country will have to change.

Having said all this about the automobile, let us not forget what a wonderful machine it is. The automobile has liberated several generations of Americans. It offers unparalleled freedom, great convenience and a very good umbrella. Over the next few years, Americans are going to have to measure their choices: to decide what emission levels are tolerable and to learn what alternative opportunities exist, and at what cost. For example, can we develop fuel-cell-driven cars, eventually powered perhaps by hydrogen combustion, that are cheap enough to be practicable and clean enough to reverse the pollution generated by the automobile? Or must we turn to public transportation, thus changing commuting, travel and consumption habits?

The answer to that last question is probably "all of the above," given the magnitude of the adverse effects of the automobile and the scale of the measures necessary to reverse them. And therein lies a key idea that we are trying to make in this book. Environmentalists tend to be very much against automobiles (though most of them still own one). Given the present realities of population and pollution, they are right. Many of them have, however, been trapped into accepting population growth as a given rather than considering it a variable that can be changed. They should be pursuing the *optimum*.

One can envisage a nation that has the use of automobiles within reason, thanks to a combination of good population policy and good technology. Fuel-cell cars, available for weekend getaways and short trips and used by those like farmers who tend to be dispersed, would work well in a country of perhaps 150 million people. They have no place in a country heading toward 400 million.

It is a matter of numbers. The idea of the automobile is not necessarily all bad. By seeing the implications of population policy, critics might legitimately contemplate a less restricted future. As the editor of *Science* put it,

> It is important to identify the main villain as overpopulation. In the good old days (viewed through the myopia of nostalgia), the water, air, flora and fauna existed in an idyllic utopia. But in truth there were famine, starvation, horses and buggies that contributed to pollution, fireplaces that spewed forth soot from burning soft coal, and water contaminated with microorganisms. The humans were so few, and the land so vast, that these insults to nature could be absorbed without serious consequences. That is no longer true.[66]

The optimal society would get rid of those fireplaces, but not be so constrained that constantly maximizing environmental efficiency was its only option. That, in a nutshell, is the difference between *optimum population* and *sustainability*.[67]

Each decade, at the present rate of population growth, we make the problem 10 percent more difficult and the time frame for the choice that much shorter.

THE EASY—AND INSUFFICIENT—"SOLUTIONS"

The traditional economist might argue that since labor produces wealth, more people means more capital to finance the transition to an environmentally sustainable economic system. This argument ignores the fact that the constraints on economic activity at the present stage of development are likely to be physical limits or the environmental impact of the activity. Agriculture is a good case in point. Diminishing crop responses, limited water availability, the pest problem and the environmental effects of fertilizer and pesticide use are the limiting factors.

More generally, the traditional economic argument simply ignores the lessons of the technological revolution. Production (particularly of goods) is no longer a function of raw labor, but rather of capital and knowledge, managed by a limited number of highly skilled people. In this regard, a major conceptual line was crossed about 15 years ago, when the economists Anne Carter and Nobel laureate Vassily Leontief, in developing an economic model for the United Nations, made output in the industrialized countries a function of capital availability rather than labor. In other words, more people do not necessarily produce more capital.

That insight is proving prescient. Around the world, unemployment has become a central economic issue. The managing director of the International Monetary Fund warns that "high and rising unemployment" is on the way to becoming a "devastating trend" in the world economy.[68] The U.S. Undersecretary of the Treasury says that the world is still gripped by "a terrible recession" and that the administration's top priority is "restoring job creation in industrial countries."[69] European Community employment ministers warn that European workers will have to take wage cuts if the Community is to create new jobs.[70]

In the United States, the number of people on food stamps reached a record 26.8 million in early 1993. The 1994 budget, in a reversal of the usual optimism of budget projections, anticipates that it will go higher.[71] The Labor Department estimates that 700,000 defense-related jobs have disappeared since 1987 and that another 1.3 million will disappear between now and 1997.[72]

Personnel cuts announced by established companies such as Boeing and IBM have brought the problem to the middle class, which is likely to be more vocal about its pain than the poor and the minorities, who so far have been the main victims. The *Wall Street Journal* quotes an estimate that "re-engineering" of production may wipe out 25 million of the 90 million jobs in the private sector in this decade. One observer says that "this may be the biggest social issue of the next 20 years."[73]

One may legitimately ask whether, in this environment, national policy should encourage an increase of job applicants, either from immigration or, later, because of high fertility.

We have observed that this country's wage and social structures are coming more and more to resemble those of the overpopulated third world countries, most of which are trying to escape their demographic plight through birth control. Let us not hasten the process of changing places with them because of some obscure doctrinal opposition to addressing P, the population factor.

Indeed, if the U.S. government's reaction to the problems of unemployment and urban unrest has been to offer Band-Aids, the official vision of the connections between population and the environment has been even less responsible.

From 1981 to 1993, the government was in the hands of certified optimists. Perhaps because it is politically dangerous to talk about population, with its minefields of immigration and fertility policy, no one did. If one does not want to address P—population—the only recourse is to pin one's faith on C—consumption—and T—technology. In short, those who prefer not to face the tough issues reach for placebos: "We must simply manage our resources better and practice conservation," or "Technology will raise productivity, as it has in the past, and provide for our needs."

Conservation

The nation must indeed practice conservation. In this consumption-driven society, conservation can be a good thing—such as shifting the American diet away from meat and feeding less cereal to livestock. However, conservation is a limited remedy. It becomes harder and harder as we move beyond the easier sacrifices. It may be well to eat less meat, but must we give it up altogether? And then, what about vegetables? And finally, cereals themselves? Conservation is a solution that wears out rapidly. When the demographer points out that U.S. population is growing nearly 10 percent each decade, the conservationist says "I can easily find ways to cut back 10 percent without real deprivation." The demographer says "What about the next generation?" and the conservationist gives the same answer, perhaps less confidently. It is a debate the conservationist cannot win. Each 10 percent gain in conserving resources is a smaller absolute gain, and the end point is zero. Meanwhile, population growth drives that inescapable formula, $I = PCT$, and wipes out those benefits of conservation.

It is all very well to berate ourselves with the charge of "consumerism" and to idealize a simpler life, but how far back in time does even the zealot want to go? There is nothing inherently wrong with wanting to have a warm house in winter or to drive a car. The problem arises when the demand grows to the point where we imperil our own environment.

Technology

As for technology, it too should certainly be employed, but with discretion. In some limited areas, application of technology may be a sufficient solution. Take the case of the threat of increased ultraviolet radiation resulting from household and industrial use of CFCs. Technology is finding substitutes for these compounds, particularly after successive Montreal Protocols ordered a phaseout of CFC production. Recent evidence suggests that emissions are declining and the rate of increase of stratospheric CFCs has slowed. It may take half a century or more to eradicate the problem, but the world is on the right track.[74]

In other areas, technology can satisfy at least part of the problem. The introduction of energy-efficient light bulbs, for instance, should make some dent in electricity consumption.

Over time, we will undoubtedly learn to do things more efficiently, and with less waste and damage. Proposals can be found today in almost every sphere of activity. A Japanese firm has even proposed a technique for converting carbon dioxide into carbohydrates through photosynthesis, thus at one stroke attacking the problem of global warming and producing the raw material for food or fuel.[75]

Our government, under considerable prodding, has been seeking to address environmental problems with technology, sometimes with real success. Control of lead emissions represents one example. Lead may have impaired the learning ability of a generation or more of children. By passing laws banning its use and requiring substitutes, the nation has brought annual emissions down from over 200,000 tons in 1970 to about 10,000 tons in 1989. Other laws have been almost as effective. Sulfur oxide emissions declined 26 percent in the same period (mostly before 1980); carbon monoxide decreased 40 percent, and particulate matter about 61 percent.[76]

One can hardly fault these improvements. The danger lies, however, in assuming that they are sufficient. Germany, it is said, has achieved a 50 percent reduction in airborne nitrogen oxide emissions in the past decade. The next 50 percent reduction will be a much greater challenge. Progress at that pace simply cannot be sustained, short of an economic collapse. As Paul Werbos has illustrated with respect to automobiles, the first gains in conservation and technology—smaller cars, proven efficiencies—are relatively easy. It becomes progressively more difficult to keep

58

up the rate of gain, and eventually one encounters physical limits to further gains.[77]

Technology is not necessarily benign. The opposite case can be better made. Don't wait for a technological "quick fix." The modern world has been riding a technological quick fix for most of this century, and it has gotten us into deep trouble. Technology has caused most of the environmental problems the industrial world presently faces. It has created the primary threats to the climate and the atmosphere.

A major task facing modern societies is to find new technologies—and the money to pay for them—to address the environmental issues that the old technology has generated.

The story of the automobile has already been told. As a convenience, or a technology, or even a way to create demand and stimulate the economy, the automobile is a miracle. As a new element in the environment, it has become a disaster.

The moral: Solutions usually create problems.

Technology is either irrelevant or harmful in addressing the problem of labor redundancy throughout the industrial world. As a result of the technological revolution, demand for unskilled labor has declined, producing a devastating effect, particularly in our cities. If it is to solve that problem, the government must eventually tackle the issues of immigration and fertility, and thereby reduce the competition for that diminishing pool of jobs. Neither T nor C will be of help here.

True believers in technology ignore the ecologists' warning that "you cannot do simply one thing." A technical fix directed toward one problem may create even graver problems elsewhere. We have cited the example of Telluride, Colorado. New, airtight wood stoves saved energy but multiplied smog and toxic chemicals in the valley. Around the country, houses have been buttoned up to conserve energy, and we have suddenly discovered the problem of indoor air pollution.

Much more serious is the case of chemicals. We have described the state of scientific ignorance concerning their environmental effects. People had uses for all those chemicals, but society hasn't begun seriously to consider the by-products of human economic activity.

The moral here, as we suggested at the start of this chapter, is that *as a nation, we don't know what we are doing.* In our present state of knowledge, proposing to solve problems with chemical quick fixes, without a far better process of foresight to look to the potential consequences, is akin to entrusting a steamroller to a blind man.[78]

Among the various objections to reliance on technology as *deus ex machina*, there are two particularly formidable arguments. First, don't count your chickens before they hatch.[79] The technologies are by no means all hatched that would solve the problems generated by growing human economies. It is an act of sheer faith to count on them to turn up. For example, the recent gains in agricultural yields are unprecedented in human history, and they have generated the serious problems described above. There is no reason to expect that we can maintain that spurt, or to believe that it can be pursued at tolerable environmental cost. (Indeed, the growth seems to be slowing down already.) Second, at some point one approaches the ridiculous. Is the entire state of Florida to be paved to provide for its exponentially growing fleet of automobiles? Can we envisage an agriculture—on eroding soil—that produces more and more tons per acre, forever, through technological innovation? Ten tons? Twenty? One hundred?

Believers in technology as a solution should perhaps reread the warning from the scientists of the National Academy and the Royal Society: it is not a sufficient solution.

Behind these proffered palliatives of conservation and technology, population change remains the driving and most intractable part of the problem. Without its being addressed, population growth simply eats up the gains from conservation and technology and leaves us with the problem undiminished and the easier solutions already used up.

One cannot squirm out of the problem. Population growth becomes a trap at some stage. Most of the third world is already in that trap, and the United States is at the cusp. Population growth cannot continue forever in a finite world—on the Earth or in the United States. The question is not "Should it stop?" but rather "*When* should it stop, and how?"

2

HOW BIG

WILL WE GET?

There is simply nothing so important to a people and its govern-
ment as how many of them there are, whether their number is
growing or declining, how they are distributed as between differ-
ent ages, sexes, and different social classes and racial and ethnic
groups, and . . . which way these numbers are moving.
Daniel P. Moynihan, "Defenders and Invaders,"
Washington Post, 13 June 1977

Population growth is related to environmental deterioration, overutilization of natural resources and a decline in
the quality of life of all Americans. Even at present population numbers, the picture is depressing. But what about
the future? The population will continue to grow—of that
we can be certain. Environmental deterioration, overutilization of natural resources and a decline in quality of life
will only continue if current demographic trends are maintained.

The 1990 census counted just over 249 million Americans, though some 6 million people may have been missed.[1]
Given current patterns of growth, we project that the nation's population will reach 279 million by the turn of the
century, and 400 million by the middle of the twenty-first
century. If conditions are bad now, what will they be like in
2020 or 2050?

Before we try to answer our own questions—When
should population growth stop? And how can it be
stopped?—let us take a look at past growth.

PAST GROWTH

At the first census, in 1790, about 4 million people were
counted in what was then the United States. Over the next

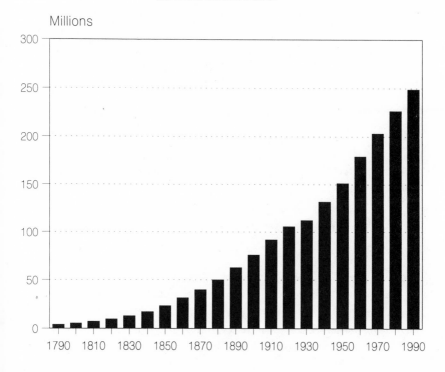

Millions

Source: *Statistical Abstract of the U.S.*, 1992.

FIGURE 2.1 *Population of the U.S.: 1790–1990*

two centuries, the population grew by just under 2 percent per year (see figure 2.1). No other country, industrialized or developing, has ever maintained such a rate for so long. Since 1950, the annual growth rate has been about 1.3 percent, the highest of any of the world's industrialized nations.

Inexplicably, some people consider this to be a low rate of growth. For example, *Washington Post* economic writer John Berry, reporting on a 1992 meeting of economists and bankers in Jackson Hole, Wyoming, noted that the "United States is in good shape, with a population growth *only* about 1.2 percent a year" (italics added).[2] (At that meeting, interestingly, N. Gregory Mankin, a Harvard economist, outlined what he called "the four secrets to fast [economic] growth." His fourth "secret" was low population growth: "If population growth is high . . . it is hard to educate the young, and without the needed skills, new workers' productivity will be low and economic growth will be slow.")

Compared to developing countries, of course, 1.2 or 1.3 percent per year is a low growth rate; compared to the European Community or Japan, however, it is exceedingly rapid. Indeed, should such a growth rate be maintained, the U.S. population would double to 500 million in a little more than fifty years and would reach one billion by the end of the twenty-first century!

What causes such growth? Simply put, for a population to grow, births must exceed deaths (natural increase) and/or the number entering the country must exceed the number leaving (net immigration).

Births have always outnumbered deaths in the United States. During the nineteenth century, when death rates fell precipitously, natural increase was particularly high. Yet the phenomenal growth of the past 200 years has not come solely from natural increase. Immigration has played a major role as well. According to demographer Campbell Gibson, over 90 percent of all Americans are the direct or indirect descendants of immigrants who came to the United States since independence in 1776.[3] To be sure, such calculations can be carried ad absurdum. Even Native Americans are the descendants of immigrants!

Nevertheless, the importance of fertility in determining population growth should not be underestimated. Even a slight shift in fertility can result in differences of millions within just a few decades. Changes in mortality also contribute to variations in population growth, with gains in life expectancy resulting in millions more people over ensuing years.

However, if we consider the direct and indirect contributions of immigration to population size, immigration as a demographic variable gains in importance. Over 8 million people moved to the United States during the first decade of the twentieth century. But their overall contribution to pop-

TABLE 2.1 *Contribution of Post-1900 Immigration*
to the Population of the U.S. in 1990

(in 000s)

If Immigration Had Ended in	1990 Pop. Would Have Been	Pop. in Specific Yr.	Immigrant Contrib. to 1990 Pop.	Total Actual Growth to 1990	% Immigrant Contrib. to 1990 Pop.
1900	174,145	76,212	74,567	172,500	43.2
1910	189,309	92,228	59,403	156,484	38.0
1920	203,795	106,022	44,917	142,690	31.5
1930	213,100	123,203	35,612	125,509	28.4
1940	214,539	132,165	34,173	116,657	29.3
1950	218,128	151,326	30,584	97,386	31.4
1960	223,400	179,323	25,312	69,389	36.5
1970	228,614	203,302	20,098	45,410	44.3
1980	238,133	226,542	10,579	22,170	47.7
1990	248,712	NA	NA	NA	NA

SOURCE: Derived from Edmonston and Passel, "The Future Immigrant Population of the United States" (Washington, D.C.: Program for Research on Immigration Policy, Urban Institute, February 1992), table 9.

ulation growth is not limited to that number. Most immigrants have children and grandchildren.

In a recent Urban Institute study, demographers Jeffrey S. Passel and Barry Edmonston demonstrated the direct and indirect contributions of immigration to population growth.[4] Let's take one example from table 2.1, which is derived from their study. Since 1960, immigration has accounted for over 36 percent of total population growth: that is, of the 69.4 million increase in population between 1960 and 1990, the immigrant contribution was 25.3 million. If immigration had ceased in 1960, therefore, the 1990 population would be 223 million rather than 249 million, and if immigration had ended in 1900, the 1990 population would be only 174 million.

Clearly, the three demographic variables—fertility, mortality and immigration—cannot be separated when dealing with population change, be it in the past, the present or the future. All must be considered in any proposed population policy.

EXISTING POPULATION PROJECTIONS

What about the twenty-first-century population of the United States? How large will it get? Will it reach 400 million, as suggested above? How much will immigration contribute to growth?

In recent years, numerous population projections for the United States have been developed. These projections, it is important to note, are neither predictions nor forecasts. (Predictions are best left to seers and psychics, forecasts to meteorologists and economists.) Rather, they are intended to answer a pointed question: How large will the population be *if certain assumptions* about fertility, mortality and migration are operable? Or more simply stated: What if . . . ? The assumptions need not be realistic. For example, according to the latest 1992 U.N. population projections, if current fertility rates remain constant for all regions, world population, now at 5.4 billion, will reach 694 billion by 2150.[5] (That is correct; it is not a typo!)

No one believes that current world population growth rates can continue indefinitely. Yet this is an accurate projection because it shows what *would* happen *if* they did.

This world projection vividly illustrates the fact that, given its carrying capacity, the planet cannot maintain the present rate of growth indefinitely. Yet such a number indicates what the population would be under certain clearly stated demographic assumptions. The "purpose of projecting population," writes Peter Morrison, "is not exclusively, or even primarily, to make accurate predictions. Rather, it is to identify and chart the likely influences and contingencies that will determine future population size."[6]

Since at least the 1940s, the Census Bureau has formulated projections of the nation's population every four or five years based on demographic trends at a given time. As demographic trends change, the bureau prepares new projections that take these changes into account.[7]

In its 1989 series of projections, no less than 27 different scenarios were constructed. Each demographic variable had high, medium and low estimates, and all combinations were projected to 2080.[8] We will look at two of its projections.

Its "middle assumption" model (series no. 14 and the model then accepted as the most likely) assumed that fertility in this country would remain constant at 1.8 live births per woman, life expectancy would eventually reach 81.2 years (for both sexes combined), and net immigration would average 500,000 annually. According to this scenario, the U.S. population would peak at 302 million in 2040 and then gradually fall, reaching 292 million by 2080. The "high assumption" model (series 9), by contrast, saw fertility rising to 2.2, life expectancy increasing to 88 years, and annual net immigration at 800,000. In 2040, the U.S. population would be 380 million; by 2080, there would be more than 500 million people living in the United States.

Demographers Dennis A. Ahlburg and James W. Vaupel sharply criticized the Census Bureau's assumptions for fertility and immigration, saying that they were too low. In their view, we could easily have a population of 811 million (near the present population of India) by 2080. They write:

A U.S. population of 800 million may seem incredible, but the annual average growth rate that produces it runs at only 1.3 percent per year. This is the same as the average annual growth rate that has prevailed in the United States over the last half-century and not too much above the 1 percent average growth rate of the last decade.[9]

In 1992, Passel and Edmonston prepared detailed population projections for the United States to 2090 that assumed annual net immigration of 950,000 and slightly higher fertility than in the Census Bureau report.[10] According to their calculations, the nation's population would reach 320 million by 2020, almost 370 million by the middle of the next century and 437 million by 2090.

In *Peaceful Invasions: Immigration and Changing America*, Leon Bouvier developed a set of projections for the nation to the year 2050.[11] He, too, assumed higher fertility and immigration than did the Census Bureau. The 2020 population of the United States, according to his medium scenario, would reach 333 million, and by 2050 there would be 388 million Americans. The high scenario projects a population of 464 million by 2050, while the low scenario projects 316 million.

Because of shifts upward in fertility and immigration after 1989, and perhaps in part because of these other nongovernmental projections, the Census Bureau revised its projections.[12] The new report, released on 4 December 1992, came as quite a surprise to many. The bureau's medium scenario, which assumes that fertility will remain constant at about 2.0 live births per woman and that annual net immigration will be 880,000, projects a population of 383 million by 2050, 134 million more people than were counted in the 1990 census—in other words, a more than 50 percent increase within 60 years. In sharp contrast to the middle scenario of the study completed a mere three years earlier, moreover, this new projection sees no end to growth. By 2045–2050, the average annual rate of growth would still be an estimated 0.49 percent. Were the calculations to be carried beyond 2050 to 2080 or 2100, the half-billion mark would be easily reached and surpassed.

In September 1993, less than a year after releasing those projections, the Census Bureau again updated its estimates.[13] Such an immediate revision is unprecedented and may reflect a profound uncertainty about the rapid demographic shifts taking place in this country. The author of the report notes, "Particularly striking in these new projections is greater growth in births in Hispanic communities and higher immigration of White, non-Hispanic persons."

Despite these new Census Bureau projections, the media expressed little concern over how such growth would affect the nation's future. This begs an obvious question: Why isn't anyone paying attention?

If nothing else, all these recent projections underscore one fact: the nation's population will continue to grow rapidly for years to come unless something dramatic happens to fertility, immigration or mortality. It is also clear that even slight shifts in these three demographic variables seriously affect population size a few decades later.

Despite the plethora of population projections, however, a special one must be constructed for this study. Not only does evidence suggest that fertility has gone up more than was previously anticipated, but recent immigration legislation has led to a growing number of people entering the country. The Immigration Act of 1990 raised the number of visas issued for occupational purposes. It also set aside 55,000 slots for diversification of the immigration stream. The law set a "cap" on total immigration—700,000 for the years 1992–1994 and 675,000 thereafter. However, this cap is flexible. Immediate family members of U.S. citizens will still be eligible to enter the country without limit; if that number rises above 220,000, the number of other family-based visas will decrease, but only to a minimum of 226,000. It is estimated that the "floor" of 226,000 visas for relatives other than spouses and children of citizens will push total admissions to 754,000 by 1996. To these must be added refugees (those seeking political or economic asylum) and illegal entries.

Illegal immigration via airplane, it now appears, may be much larger than previously thought.[14] And the use of asylum has certainly intensified in recent years. Indeed, the number of persons claiming asylum—many without proper reasons—has become so large that the United States is now interdicting ships off the Atlantic and Pacific coasts so as to prevent such "asylees" from coming ashore. "Under U.S. law," an article in Newsweek entitled "Playing the Asylum Game" stated, "claiming asylum prevents the INS [Immigration and Naturalization Service] from deporting you right away. The reason is that everyone on U.S. soil—even foreign citizens—has the legal right to full due process under the Constitution."[15] Thus, with net immigration levels increasing to at least 1 million annually, special projections must be prepared to demonstrate the effects of this immigration on overall population growth.

These assumptions reflect what we believe are current trends in demographic behavior. Nevertheless, the projection is just that: it indicates what the population of the United States might be in specific years according to stated assumptions about fertility, mortality and migration. While alternative scenarios will be offered later, only one projection is discussed here. We are concerned with two questions: What will the future population of the United States be if current demographic behavior continues? And what will be the relative effect of immigration on population growth?

Our base for this projection is the U.S. population in the year 2000, which we estimate will be 279.1 million. We then project the nation's population for the entire twenty-first century, but emphasizing the first half-century more than the last. Since we want to illustrate the impact of future immigration on population size, two separate "populations" are developed: U.S. residents as of 2000 and their descendants, and post-2000 immigrants and their descendants. In that way, it will be easy to see the relative contribution of immigration to overall population size in any given year. (The detailed assumptions of our model are discussed in the appendix.)

U.S. POPULATION GROWTH: A NEW PROJECTION

Given current demographic trends, as best as they can be determined, the U.S. population will reach 300 million in about 2012, 350 million in 2025 and 397 million by 2050 (see table 2.2 and figure 2.2). Between 1990 and 2050, in other words, the United States will have added almost 150 million people—approximately equal to the total U.S. population in 1950. Its average annual rate of growth will be about 0.8 percent.

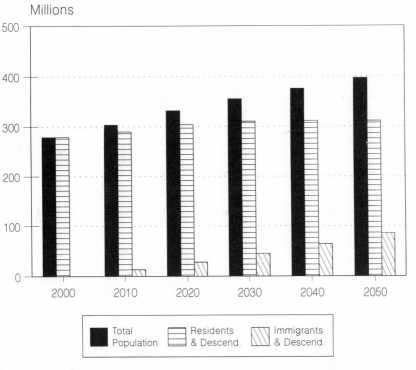

FIGURE 2.2 *Projected Population of the U.S.: 2000–2050*

Is nearly 400 million Americans in 2050 an exaggerated "prediction"? Are we resorting to scare tactics here? The projections discussed earlier suggest otherwise. A population of 400 million Americans by mid-century is quite probable—again, given current demographic trends.

Over the 50-year period under discussion, the resident population will increase by only 32 million (from 279 million in 2000 to 311 million in 2050), peaking in 2040 and then beginning a very slow decline. This pattern is explained by the assumed total fertility rate of 2.0—just below the level needed to replace the population in the long run. After 2040, deaths will exceed births in the residents-and-descendants group.

The real driving force in U.S. population growth, therefore, is immigration. In table 2.3 we have calculated the

TABLE 2.2 Projected Population of the U.S.: 2000–2050
(in 000s)

Year	Year 2000 Residents and Descendants	Post-2000 Immigrants and Descendants	Total
2000	279,146	NA	279,146
2010	292,017	13,171	305,188
2020	304,131	27,992	332,123
2030	310,546	45,040	355,586
2040	311,635	64,474	376,109
2050	311,470	85,462	396,932

TABLE 2.3 U.S. Population in 2050
if Immigration Ended in Specific Year
(in 000s)

Year Immigration Ends	Year 2000 Residents and Descendants	Post-2000 Immigrants and Descendants	Total Population in 2050
2000	311,470	NA	311,470
2010	311,470	23,862	335,332
2020	311,470	43,105	354,575
2030	311,470	59,665	371,135
2040	311,470	73,893	385,363
2050	311,470	85,462	396,932

2050 population based on various immigration cut-off points over the 2000–2050 period. For example, if immigration ended in 2010, the 2050 population would be only 335 million (versus 397 million if immigration were maintained over the entire time span). If immigration did end in 2010, the 10 million immigrants entering between 2000 and 2010 would lead to almost 24 million people by 2050. This again illustrates the powerful indirect contribution of immigration to population growth.

If immigration does *not* stop during this 50-year period, the immigrants-and-descendants group will grow even faster than the actual level of immigration because of that group's higher-than-replacement fertility. That is, the 50 million immigrants (again, 1 million annually) will actually contribute over 85 million people to the population of 2050. Thus, the direct and indirect effects of immigration between 2000 and 2050 account for 72 percent of total growth, with the higher fertility of immigrants contributing to a higher overall fertility rate.

The tendency for immigrants to have larger families than their native-born counterparts has been referred to as "shifting shares."[16] Whenever two subgroups of a population exhibit different fertility levels, the one having the higher fertility increases its share of the total population at the expense of the group with lower fertility. As a result, the fertility of the overall population will increase over the long run even if the fertility of each subgroup remains constant. Under these conditions, in other words, immigration increases the fertility rate in the host country.

Age Distribution

The average age of the U.S. population will continue to increase in future years. In 2000, a little over 11 percent of the population will be 65 or over, about the same as in 1990. That proportion will expand to 17.5 percent in 2030 when the baby boomers will have all become senior citizens, and to 18.4 percent in 2050. Over the 50-year period, therefore, the number of elderly will more than double, from 31 million to 73 million.

When a society exhibits low fertility, as has been true of the United States for the past two decades, population aging usually occurs; that is, the proportion of the elderly grows while that of the young falls. As a result, the dependency ratio (the number of persons age 0–14 and 65 + per 100 persons age 15–64) does not vary much; the emphasis merely shifts from youth dependency to aging dependency.

This will not be the case for the United States in the first

TABLE 2.4 *Projected Age Composition of the U.S.: 2000–2050*

	2000		2030		2050	
Age	No. (in 000s)	%	No. (in 000s)	%	No. (in 000s)	%
0–14	61,095	(21.9)	70,430	(19.8)	78,004	(19.7)
15–64	186,353	(66.8)	222,881	(62.7)	245,843	(61.9)
65+	31,698	(11.3)	62,275	(17.5)	73,085	(18.4)
Dependency Ratio	49.7		59.4		61.5	

half of the twenty-first century (see table 2.4). While the elderly share will rise from 11.3 to 18.4 percent, the youth share will fall only slightly, from 21.9 to 19.7 percent. As a consequence, the dependency ratio will rise significantly: from 49.7 "dependents" per 100 "active" persons in 2000, to 61.5 in 2050.

This somewhat unanticipated situation has two primary causes: (1) the baby boom that lasted from 1947 to 1964 will contribute to a relatively rapid aging of the population as these people begin entering retirement in about 2015; and (2) because immigrants are generally young adults, they are projected to have fairly high fertility at least for the early decades of the next century. Thus, in this country, the share of youths will not drop as rapidly as it does when immigration is not a major contributor to population growth.

Labor Force Impact

To illustrate the significance of this change, let's examine the population age 20–24, the cohort with the greatest incremental impact on the labor force. The total numbers of this group will rise from 19 million in 2000 to 25.2 million in 2050. As table 2.5 shows, however, that growth will come from immigration rather than from natural increase among residents. In fact, the age 20–24 residents-and-descendants population will be smaller in 2050 than in 2000. Needless to say, such growth, especially coming as it does mainly

TABLE 2.5 *Projected Population of the U.S.,*
Age 20–24: 2000 to 2050

(in 000s)

Year	Year 2000 Residents and Descendants	Post-2000 Immigrants and Descendants	Total
2000	18,875	186	19,061
2010	21,306	1,162	22,468
2020	19,503	2,038	21,541
2030	19,242	3,751	22,993
2040	19,500	5,042	24,542
2050	18,821	6,427	25,248

from immigration, could lead to increased unemployment as well as further social and economic problems in the nation's large cities, where immigrants congregate.

Ethnic Shifts

Although in this book we are primarily concerned with how immigration, per se, contributes to population growth and how, in turn, such growth relates to quality of life, we would be remiss not to mention the broad changes that will occur in the ethnic composition of the United States in the twenty-first century.

Over time, as we have seen, post-2000 immigrants and their descendants will make up an ever greater share of the total number of Americans—from 4.5 percent of the population in 2010, to 21.5 percent by 2050. The middle scenario of the most recent Census Bureau projections, moreover, indicates that in 2050 non-Hispanic Whites (or "Anglos") will constitute 52.7 percent of the U.S. population, while the shares for Hispanics, African-Americans, and Asians and Others will be 21.1, 15.0 and 11.2 percent, respectively. Bouvier, in *Peaceful Invasions*, arrives at similar numbers. (See figure 2.3 for comparative depictions of the year 2000 and the year 2050.)[17] Although our demo-

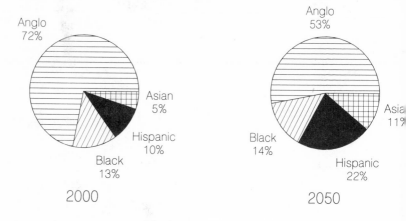

Source: Bouvier, *Peaceful Invasions.*

FIGURE 2.3 *Projected Population of the U.S. by Ethnicity: 2000 and 2050*

graphic assumptions differ somewhat from those used in *Peaceful Invasions*, we agree with them and the Census Bureau's projections for ethnic composition in 2050.

To sum up: the United States of 2050 will differ considerably from the United States of today. Its population will be older; it will be ethnically more diverse. Most important, its population will be approaching the 400 million mark—some 150 million more than that enumerated in the most recent census.

BEYOND 2050

The longer the time frame, the more tenuous the projection. We are far more confident of the period 2000–2050 than of the period 2050–2100. The University of Texas demographer Parker Frisbie wryly comments, "Anyone who speculates on what the future holds is well-advised to concentrate on dates as far removed from the present as possible, since the longer the prognostication interval, the fewer the number of critics who will remember and point out errant predictions."[18] With this in mind, let us briefly examine that more distant period, still looking at the effect of current demographic trends if they were to remain constant, in this

TABLE 2.6 *Projected Population of the U.S.: 2050–2100*
(in 000s)

Year	Year 2000 Residents and Descendants	Post-2000 Immigrants and Descendants	Total Population	Total if Immigration Ended in 2050
2050	311,470	85,462	396,932	396,932
2060	310,603	107,265	417,868	406,302
2070	307,871	129,328	437,199	411,649
2080	304,720	151,540	456,260	414,924
2090	301,631	173,266	474,897	416,076
2100	298,204	193,946	492,150	415,085

case for another century. It will then be up to the American people to decide if such a future is desirable or not and, if not, whether to take action to render these projections incorrect.

Population growth over the last half of the twenty-first century will probably be somewhat slower than in the first half, reaching perhaps 492 million by the year 2100—a gain of less than 100 million in 50 years (table 2.6). This lower growth rate can be explained by a decline in the fertility rate among post-2000 immigrants and their descendants. By 2050, we assume that the rate will have fallen from 2.7 (in 2000) to 2.3; by 2100, it will reach 2.0.

The group comprising residents in 2000 and their descendants will continue the numerical decline first noted just prior to 2050: from 311 million in that year, their total will drop gradually to 298 million in 2100. By contrast, the post-2000 immigrants-and-descendants group will grow from 85 million in 2050 to 194 million in 2100.

We also calculated what would happen to eventual population size if immigration came to an end in 2050 (table 2.6). By 2100, instead of 492 million, the total U.S. population would be only 415 million. Indeed, by 2090 a very slow decline would have begun.

Given the low fertility anticipated, the aging process will

continue through the latter decades of the next century. By 2100, 19.4 percent of the American population will be 65 or over, and almost as many (18.9 percent) will be under 15. The resulting dependency ratio will remain a relatively high 62.1.

Significantly, all growth after 2040 results from the direct and indirect effects of twenty-first-century immigration. If the sources of future immigration approximate those currently noted, the United States of 2100 will be unrecognizable to Americans of today. Not only will it be approaching the half-billion mark in population, but it will also be much older (almost one in five will be elderly), and it will be far more racially diverse. Of course, there is nothing wrong with an older, more heterogeneous society. Nonetheless, such demographic shifts pose serious challenges for the nation. For example, the health-care issues associated with a doubling of the elderly population will be enormous, as will be the educational challenge of preparing the non-English-speaking children of immigrants for their proper role in twenty-first-century American society.

Will these projections become reality in the next century? Will there be 400 million Americans in 2050? Half a billion in 2100? We don't know. Demographic trends have been known to shift abruptly and dramatically. Demographers of the 1930s or even early 1940s did not foresee a baby boom that would last almost two decades. While an end to the baby boom was expected, the length of the so-called baby bust era (1972 to about 1988) was unanticipated. Future baby booms are certainly possible, though unlikely. For that matter, fertility could fall back to late-1970s levels.

Mortality rates are far more stable. Yet even here, unexpected changes have occurred in the past. For example, the life expectancy of male African-Americans has actually fallen in recent years. And no one knows what the future holds. Will the AIDS epidemic reach enormous proportions? Will environmental damage, associated with population growth, contribute to high mortality? Then again, the tremendous achievements in recent medical research and public health policy could mean longer life spans than ever before.

Even immigration, which can be manipulated through federal legislation, has proven to be highly volatile. The immigration legislation of 1965 resulted in massive movements in the 1970s and 1980s. Yet when it was passed, most politicians were convinced that its impact would be negligible. In arguing for the act, then-Attorney General Robert F. Kennedy told the Senate that 5,000 Asian immigrants might come the first year, "after which immigration from that source would virtually disappear."[19] Present prospects are that the rapid population growth expected in typical sending countries will cause immigration levels to climb in the next century. In the face of public pressure, though, Congress could be motivated to pass restrictive legislation, which might conceivably be effectively enforced.

In this chapter we have attempted to look at current demographic trends and project what these might lead to in the next century. Given such trends, a population of 400 million is highly possible by 2050, as is half a billion by 2100. We don't need to stoop to scare tactics to convince people that the nation has a population problem. Many population projections, drawn up by many experts, point in the same direction.

As of this writing, the United States is headed down that road, demographically. From 279 million in 2000, it could reach almost 500 million a mere 100 years later. What will such growth mean for our environment?

3

THE COST OF DOING NOTHING

In 1917 the total number of Americans passed 100 million, after three full centuries of steady growth. In 1967—just half a century later—the 200 million mark was passed. If the present rate of growth continues, the third hundred million persons will be added in roughly a thirty-year period. This means that by the year 2000, or shortly thereafter, there will be more than 300 million Americans.

The growth will produce serious challenges for our society. I believe that many of our present social problems may be related to the fact that we have had only fifty years in which to accommodate the second hundred million Americans. . . .

Where, for example, will the next hundred million Americans live? . . .

How will we educate and employ such a large number of people? Will our transportation systems move them about as quickly and economically as necessary? How will we provide adequate health care when our population reaches 300 million? Will our political structures have to be reordered, too, when our society grows to such proportions? . . .

. . . We should establish as a national goal the provision of adequate family planning services within the next five years to all those who want them but cannot afford them.

Richard M. Nixon, "Special Message to the U.S. Congress
on Problems of Population Growth," July 18, 1969

We are approaching that 300 million mark, a little behind schedule because the baby boom ended more abruptly than expected. We are now looking beyond that projection toward a population passing 400 million in just over two generations and pushing 500 million in a century. We have not, however, answered the questions that President Nixon posed, and now, nearly a quarter of a century later, his speech sounds prophetic.

The figures in chapter 2 are projections, not destiny. The numbers may be lower if American women decide to have fewer children, or if conditions in this country deteriorate enough to discourage immigration, as happened during the Great Depression. On the other hand, the numbers could be much higher.

The point is that substantial growth is the direction in which we are heading, and it would be dangerous policy indeed simply to wait and hope that the problem will just go away. In human affairs, problems don't always go away. The path to overpopulation is insidious. Within the lifetime of the authors, the population of India has climbed from less than 300 million to nearly 900 million and is heading past one billion. China was 500 million or less (nobody really knows) and is now well past one billion, despite heroic efforts to stop population growth. The United States is moving into that league.

THE RATE OF GROWTH

The projected growth in our scenario (chapter 2) works out to about 8 percent each decade, or just under 0.8 percent per year, from 1990 through 2050. To readers used to mortgage rates, or even rates of inflation, that rate may seem low. Indeed, it is lower than the country's historical growth rate during any one decade in its history (which in itself perhaps suggests that our projection is very conservative). Nevertheless, it leads to the numbers detailed in the preceding chapter. It may therefore be useful to examine, as best we can, the effects that such population growth is likely to have on the issues described in chapter 1.

These forecasts can only be conjectural, since we cannot know whether the nation will adjust to the population growth by reducing per capita consumption, or whether there will be increasing chaos as the prosperous stake their claim to more and more of the pie, the poor get poorer and the country becomes more like India. Further, since we cannot predict the effects of techniques and processes that have not yet been discovered, we have no way of knowing how much help the country will receive from technology. Never-

theless, it is worth making some projections based on recent experience, now that the technological revolution has
matured and some of the attendant problems have come to
light.

THE WEIGHT OF NUMBERS

We have observed that the population issue can be looked at
in two ways: from the standpoint of the sheer numbers
involved, and in terms of the problems that population
growth itself generates, which may be quite distinct from
absolute size per se. Because the effect of total numbers is
perhaps more readily grasped, we will deal with it first.

The Cities

In 1981, during a prolonged drought, it was reported that
sewage effluent had come to constitute 55 to 70 percent of
the flow of the Passaic River, which provides the household
and drinking water for about 2.2 million residents of north-
ern New Jersey. The authorities tripled the chlorination rate
and pronounced the water fit to drink, although it was said
to foam as it came from the tap and "taste like bleach," and
there were unanswered questions as to the health effects of
the chlorine compounds created by all that chlorine as it
mixed with natural organics in the water.[1]

More urban residents will be drinking chlorinated sewage by 2050 if the population rises by the projected 60 percent. A few cities have adequate long-term water supplies,
though even New York, with its vast watershed in the Cats-
kills, has been forced to ration water from time to time and
is now facing the need for an immense water treatment
plant as population grows in those mountains and contam-
inates the city's water supply.[2] Cities like Los Angeles, benefiting from new legislation, will take water from irrigation,
thus hastening the decline of California agriculture. Others,
dependent on limited river flows or groundwater, will not
be so fortunate.

In the 1970s, the nation began an $18 billion program of
support for sewage treatment plants and interceptor sewers

to stop the eutrophication of our rivers and the Great Lakes with raw sewage. Even so, the overall problem of sewage sludge disposal gets worse. Nitrates, phosphates and toxic chemicals and metals pour into rivers and coastal waters, wiping out fisheries and making downstream stretches of the rivers less and less usable for humans. Already in 1990 the taking of fish and shellfish was limited or banned in 37 percent of our estuarial waters. In Louisiana alone, the areas declared off-limits had increased by 46 percent in five years. The "solution" for coastal cities has been to pump sludge farther out at sea. Ocean sludge dumping almost doubled from 1973 to 1987, when it reached 8.7 million tons. Thus the nation proceeds to degrade the oceans as it has the land.[3]

In this area, clearly, we are hitting the limits. Sewage sludge is related to total numbers of people in a singularly inelastic fashion. More use can and must be made of treated sewage in agriculture, if the toxicity problem can be ameliorated, but even that solution is not without flaws. Urban sludge and agriculture are the two major culprits in the degradation of surface waters and groundwater, and runoff will occur even if the sludge is put on agricultural land. In this instance, we are simply overtaxing the ability of natural systems to handle our effluent, and there is no economical process for sequestering it. A 60 percent intensification of an already worsening problem is a grim thought indeed.

As we saw in chapter 1, the problem of urban solid waste disposal is already out of control. If recent experience is a guide, most of the projected 60 percent population growth by 2050 will occur in metropolitan areas. The effort to handle the added numbers will require compulsory (and expensive) recycling, more incineration (which will require expensive environmental controls) and the creation of major new dumps in isolated areas (to which waste will be carted over long distances—again, at considerable expense). Coastal cities will be under intense pressure to go back to dumping at sea, despite the strictures of the Ocean Dumping Convention. In any event, such a reversion will buy only a little time by extending the area of our impact. The sea is not infinite, and we have already catalogued some of the damage that human activity is inflicting on the marine environment. A 60 percent increase in the trash load is not a happy prospect.

Other urban problems are hardly less daunting. The cities have fallen far behind in maintenance and repair, as the resident knows and the visiting driver soon learns. The neglect extends to most older cities and most infrastructure: roads, bridges that occasionally fall down, public buildings, water systems and storm and sanitary sewer systems.

Part of the problem is the need for additional investment to accommodate growth (see below), but part is simply the result of bigness. In the major cities, the physical crowding of streets and even sidewalks is already serious (try Manhattan at noon or rush hour). It cannot be ameliorated except by destroying the city itself through massive demolition and displacement, because the buildings are already in place. The cost will be enormous, probably involving the subsidized construction of subways. An additional burden of 60 percent or more people will impose dramatic new strains on the very fabric of the cities. And no amount of investment will be able to reduce the physical crowding then.

Automobiles particularly afflict the cities, because of the space they demand, the pollution they create and their disruption of the human scale of the city. With the projected population increase, in 2050 we will be worse off than we are now even if one out of three users gives up driving.

Energy

While not so painfully apparent, the problems of energy use are, if anything, more serious. We argued in chapter 1 that the present pattern of U.S. energy use is simply unsustainable, with or without a population increase. Environmental constraints, balance of payments difficulties, the risks of relying on a distant and unstable region for our basic energy requirements, the worldwide competition for remaining fossil energy supplies and the fact that no known fossil energy source will meet world demands for very long in any case all combine to make the point that we must get on with the energy transition.

Particularly in the transportation sector, the transition is going to be epochal. It is not likely to be simply a question of shifting to little cars driven by fuel cells powered by hydrogen derived from solar energy, as futuristic magazine articles suggest from time to time. Even if the private automobile survives in some form and numbers, the entire support system must change: the service stations, pipelines, repair services, probably our living and commuting arrangements, the distribution of retail and service establishments now reached by private automobile, parks, recreation facilities and vacation patterns. A whole generation of workers in the transportation industry must be retrained.

There will be other changes as well. Energy will almost certainly be more expensive. A power company official familiar with the Cool Water low-pollution coal generation pilot facility (see chapter 1) said that it was closed down because it simply could not compete with petroleum at any price below $40 per barrel, even with the capital costs already written off.

If that energy is expensive, benign energy such as direct solar conversion with silicon wafers on an industrial scale is even more so. Such approaches are still far from competitive even for peaking power. Southern California Edison currently buys almost 30 percent of the power it supplies from alternative energy sources.[4] They pay $0.15 per kilowatt-hour for solar energy, $0.11 for wind and biomass-generated power, and about $0.06 for power from small hydro plants, cogeneration by industry, and geothermal energy, for an average of $0.08. Compare that with the $0.03 it costs them to generate power from gas or petroleum.

These newer technologies, of course, tend to be at a small and relatively primitive state, and their prices have been going down. Nevertheless, the comparative figures do give an early reading on what we may expect of the more benign technologies. On the one hand, it is encouraging that power can be produced from renewable sources at prices that are at least within sight. On the other hand, power in the future will likely be more expensive than now, and the solar and wind technologies are ill suited to provide baseline power.

Rising energy costs will increase the attractions of the Sun Belt, with its lower heating costs and higher potential for solar heating and household power. These advantages may accelerate a migration already under way.

This is a fundamental restructuring, and it is not made easier by adding 8 percent per decade to the population to be supplied with energy.

Agriculture

We have identified the problems facing agriculture: diminishing response to fertilizers; rising losses due to pests, especially in monoculture crops; depleted aquifers and the loss of irrigation water to urban uses; vulnerability to rising energy prices; erosion of the best topsoil.

For the United States, these problems are not as immediate as those involving energy, but they warn of a plateau or even decline in yields, which in the long term is far more serious than the energy transition. The issues of erosion, the diminishing effectiveness of pesticides and loss of genetic variety foretell even more trouble ahead.

Agricultural exports have been a workhorse in the U.S. balance of payments. Even though we have been importing more, we still run an annual surplus of $9 billion to $19 billion in our agricultural trade. The margin of U.S. agricultural production over domestic requirements is not, however, very wide. It fluctuates with each year's harvest, but in the late 1980s it stood at 21 percent.[5] At the projected rate of population growth, just 26 years' increase will eat up that margin and wipe out our export surplus if yields should stop climbing. From then on we will be looking for imports that other countries cannot supply and we cannot afford to buy.

Of course, the increase in yields is unlikely to stop abruptly. Moreover, simpler diets and the expansion of acreage will probably defer the day of zero net exports. Nonetheless, acreage expansion means going back onto less productive and more erosive soils, and it takes land back from forests, making our forestry and biodiversity problems that much worse. It also appropriates land for food production that might have been producing biomass energy. These things are interconnected, and we are running out of margin.

It would take a true believer to bet on continuing—and sufficient—increases in yields given the problems just described. In effect, it is betting against the population Juggernaut: you may win for a half-century, but ultimately the sheer numbers of people will overtax what agriculture can produce.

Forests

Forests in the western United States are declining in the face of current demand. Although Eastern forests have now grown back in those fields and pastures that were released by the westward shift of agriculture and the replacement of the horse by the tractor, the present trend is to cut into those forests to make way for population expansion, and there is no way but down. The pine plantations in the South are the only exception, but they are producing high yields through fertilization and monoculture, which is as dangerous with trees as it is with corn.

With the official data showing a 21 percent decline in standing timber per capita from 1952 to 1987 (chapter 1)— data that many consider dangerously optimistic—and with the last big stands of old-growth rain forest in peril, a scarcity exists that is already reflected in rising lumber prices. The impact of another 140 million consumers by 2050 is self-evident.

Given a chance, the forests will grow back. Replanting is now being practiced on some, but not all, of the acreage being logged (though in some cases, such as efforts to reseed clear-cut Ponderosa stands in the mountain West, restoration is not working as planned). Still, an acre of seedlings is a far cry from an acre of harvestable timber. The nation will be in for a very tight period as replanting in the West matures, even if population growth should slow or stop.

More important is another question: What kind of forests will we have? The plants and animals that inhabit a mature forest can survive forest fires and limited cutting, but wholesale destruction of their habitat means that many species will not be around to welcome the return of mature trees. The plight of Eastern migratory songbirds, caught between the disappearance of their winter habitat in Central America and the fragmentation of forests in the northeastern United States, is a portent.

Biodiversity

The forests' condition is just one part of the larger issue of biodiversity. We made the case in chapter 1 that, with human disturbance of the biosphere that supports us at a historic peak, perhaps the most pressing of all tasks is to preserve natural systems against further destruction. Continued population growth will only impede such an effort, because it increases the demand for food, for lumber, for energy to run the system and keep us warm, and for all the other economic products whose manufacture drives the destruction of the natural world. Against the political power of the demand for "more," the appeal to protect the biosphere comes to seem a rather distant abstraction.

THE IMPACT OF POPULATION CHANGE

Let us look now at the problems generated by growth itself, aside from the eventual numbers.

The Problem of Capital

Speaking of abstractions: the idea of "capital" and its importance may sound to the reader like a rather arcane matter for the economists. Nothing could be further from the truth.

If the society is to deal with the problems already generated by economic growth, and to reform its economic practices to avoid further damage, the capital requirements are enormous. In chapter 1 we detailed some of the bills already outstanding: cleaning up nuclear and hazardous wastes; finding and financing ways of handling solid wastes and sewage sludge; managing the energy transition away from petroleum and eventually all fossil fuels; rebuilding and maintaining the physical plant of the cities; internalizing the "externalities" in manufacturing, agriculture, power generation and transportation that drive pollution; generating benign economic growth sufficient to permit employment of the working-age population. This is an intimidating list for a nation with net private savings amounting to only 4 percent of GNP and with a government unwilling to finance even its current requirements, as evidenced by our persistent budget deficits.

There is always competition between the need for capital for social infrastructure, on the one hand, and capital for "productive" investment, on the other, and that competition is intensified by population growth. The nation needs capital for social infrastructure if we are not to suffer a decline in the per capita availability of classrooms, colleges, hospitals, police departments, roads, parks, urban water supplies, sewage treatment plants and all the other requirements of a modern urbanized society. This bill goes up if the number of people to be served is rising. At the same time, business investment must also grow to provide the added numbers of people with jobs. Indeed, it must grow faster than population, if labor productivity is to rise and allow better lives for workers.

This competition is further intensified when, as at present, capital is needed to deal with postponed environmental and resource problems. We believe that a central advantage of stopping population growth (and one overlooked by most commentators on population) is that it frees resources for productive investment in the tasks that lie ahead, such as the energy transition, by holding down social infrastructure costs and applying them to a smaller population base. For example, $1 million applied to educating 200 students will be more likely to develop them into productive adults than if it is applied to 400 students.

California and Florida, where recent growth has been most extreme, provide the best lessons as to the look of the future. In 1963, California surpassed New York to become the nation's largest state. What joy in the Golden State! What anguish in the Empire State! Between 1980 and 1990, California gained seven additional seats in the U.S. Congress, all because of the continuing rise in population. But what about the downside of such monumental growth?

Overcrowded classrooms, clogged freeways, unemployment and related cultural clashes, increasingly severe water shortages, environmental decay—all derive to a certain extent from one common cause: overpopulation. While other factors have contributed to California's mounting problems, overpopulation is clearly a major component. Marginal cost is rising faster than average cost. In response to this state of affairs, *Sacramento Bee* columnist Dan Walters recently issued a challenge:

> What's needed is the creation of a state population/development policy. We need to decide what level of development we want, including population size, that's consistent with maintenance of the quality of Californians' lives and adopt strategies that will implement that goal.[6]

Florida is another example of rampant growth. In 1940, its population was less than 2 million; it has now surpassed 13 million. Perhaps more than any other state, Florida has relied almost exclusively on population growth to steer its economy. For many years, that plan worked quite well as the state collected ample sales taxes from new retirees and the millions of tourists who visited every year, both groups drawing their income from other states. As the population continued to expand, however, the state could not keep up with the demands for services. Each day, as Florida grows, nearly two miles of expanded highways, two new class-rooms, two new teachers, two additional police officers, one more local jail cell and two more state prison beds are needed. Each day, as Florida grows, 111,108 additional gallons of water are used, 94,560 additional gallons of waste water are produced, and 3,546 additional pounds of solid waste are treated. Each day, as Florida grows, services are needed for 14 more children in subsidized day care, 3 more children who are developmentally disabled, 19 more applicants for Aid for Families with Dependent Children, 38 more recipients of Medicaid, 13 more people suffering a mental illness and 70 more persons in need of alcohol and drug abuse treatment.[7]

Because Florida's public infrastructure has been unable to keep pace with the rapid population growth the state has experienced, levels of service per person have worsened.

> Unless a greater investment is made in the infrastructure, the future population growth projected for Florida means that levels of service will continue to deteriorate. This will reduce the quality of life and render the government ineffective in delivering needed services to Floridians.[8]

It is not simply a question of providing twice as many hospital beds when the population doubles. The society not only needs to build new facilities; it must also invest money to counter depreciation, that is, to repair damage and replace things that wear out. The alternative is dramatically illustrated by the condition of New York City, where a major capital structure, the West Side elevated highway, developed holes in the pavement. The highway was simply closed off to traffic through the primitive device of putting battered oil drums in the approach roads. That is decadence.

As the economy has expanded, the infrastructure has grown, and with it the annual requirements for maintenance and replacement. Our nation will need to invest more heavily in counteracting depreciation if such examples as the West Side highway closure are not to become commonplace. On top of that, a growing population requires that the infrastructure continue to expand, which means that it must find much more money for investment, simply to keep up, than does a stationary one.

The Energy Example

Chapter 1 demonstrates the compounding effect of population growth, depreciation and the need to face the environmental bills already outstanding. Readers will recall the finding that the problem of acid precipitation would be dramatically lowered if old power plants were to be replaced with new, cleaner ones on a 40-year cycle rather than a 70-year one. Very well, but consider the costs. There are nearly 700 million kilowatts of installed electric generating capacity in the United States.[9] The construction costs of new electric generating capacity are perhaps $2,000 per kilowatt, including pollution control equipment and depending on the technology used.[10] A "business as usual" 70-year cycle, using current technologies, requires new construction of 10 million kilowatts annually, or about $20 billion. On a 40-year cycle, the annual cost would go up to about $35 billion. If one of the new techniques for reducing the release of sulfates (such as the Cool Water integrated coal gasification process) were used, the cost would be substantially higher, perhaps something like $60 billion. This would substantially reduce air pollution and acid rain but do nothing to mitigate the greenhouse effect.

If we must provide power for a population expanding at an annual rate of 0.8 percent, another 5.6 million kilowatts, or about $18 billion, will be required each year.

And that is not enough. Technology still cannot ameliorate the impact of coal burning on climate. Moreover, even coal supplies will not last forever; indeed, by 2050 the end will be coming into sight. The costs of facing those facts and shifting toward truly sustainable and non-polluting technologies are still incalculable, but they are almost certain to be higher than simply replacing superannuated coal-fired power plants. One thing we do know: population growth will add 0.8 percent per year, 8 percent per decade, and 60 percent by 2050, to the energy costs of the transition.

We pointed out in chapter 1 that it is not enough to say that "people can simply conserve energy." In 2050, if the investment is not made to accommodate population growth, the energy supply per capita will be only 62.5 percent what it was in 1990. The question then will be: What do we do now to meet the needs of the 100 million more people expected by 2100?

THE PLIGHT OF THE POOR

We have mentioned the urban problems that make life miserable for people stuck at the bottom of the economic heap. Let us look specifically at unemployment and social unrest and their connection with population growth.

As we have seen, technological change has been contributing to a long-term rise in unemployment in the United States, which particularly affects unskilled youth attempting to enter the labor force. There are now some 23 to 27 million illiterate Americans, and another 40 million who are only marginally literate, trying to find work in a technically sophisticated market that demands numerous skills.[11] Young people in their early twenties, when finding a job is critical to one's future, often become so frustrated that they drop out of the labor force entirely. In 1990, the proportion of young people who are out of school but do not have full-time jobs was 50 percent for African-Americans (up from 48 percent the year before), 38 percent for Hispanics, and 30 percent for non-Hispanic Whites.[12]

Society, and the poor themselves, would benefit if fewer people were entering the 20–24 age group. The small Depression cohorts found it a lot easier to get work than did the baby boomers. And as the model in chapter 2 suggests, the age 20–24 cohort will grow by one-third by 2050. More old workers will be leaving the labor force as well, but their departure is an exchange of skilled for unskilled labor, and the young will still need to be trained. In short, things will get worse.

In chapter 5 we will offer a dramatic comparison between the way we are heading and the way we could be heading, in bringing the poor into the economic mainstream.

THE WAY WE WILL LIVE

By and large, when futurists describe the country in decades to come, they portray a beguiling idyll of clean cities surrounded by green space, of electronic miracles and cars that drive themselves. They seldom consider the numbers involved, the population dynamics or the cost of repairing the damage the nation is doing to itself. They assume that new technological wonders will be made available and take care of everything. One gets the feeling that they have not spent much time in the inner cities, or plotted the curve along which the nation is presently headed.

Recent directions will probably define future directions if we let demography take its own course. The cities have been deteriorating, and current immigration and fertility patterns suggest that they will get worse and their inhabitants more desperate. Joblessness, idleness, alienation and violence are skyrocketing, especially among the young. Urban services from health care to the removal of wastes are failing. The inner cities will become even more crowded than the national population projections indicate, because fewer people will be able to afford the luxury of the suburbs.

At this rate, how do we expect to afford those dream cities?

Across the country, our agricultural, forestry, and fishery resources are being drawn down. The most one can say so far for the brave efforts of the Clinton administration to protect rangeland and old-growth forests is that they will slow—not stop—the destruction. We face an imminent energy transition and dwindling petroleum resources, yet Congress riotously shouted down the President's modest energy tax proposal, which would have gone a small way to making renewable energy sources more competitive. This lack of foresight makes it pretty certain that we will not work through a gradual energy transition, but rather will be faced with more and worse energy crises somewhere down the road.

To put all this in blunter language: if the nation insists on staying the present course, we will be living the simple life in 2050—and it won't be as attractive as the old song suggests. We won't have cars, and without the physical security that cars provide, we won't be venturing out much in that turbulent society, particularly at night, except as part of an armed group. We will be paying high taxes for such security protection as is available, and for getting the poisons out of the air we breathe, the water we drink and the food we eat.

The gap between rich and poor is already widening. Depending on who wins—the poor or the rich—either we will descend to "third world" conditions of a tiny rich elite surrounded by the impoverished poor, or we will be forced to spread the scarcities. If the nation goes the first route and preserves conspicuous consumption for the rich—like private jets and those silly green golf courses in the Southwest that are irrigated to make them look like Kentucky—we may reasonably expect a revolution. People are not very docile these days. If we go the other route, we may expect a lot more controls on the way we live; crowded societies, after all, have little room for individual choice. We will drink the sewage from the neighbors upstream, testing for toxins, or buy bottled drinking water and hope it's safe. If we are lucky, we will have paid a lot for new forms of energy to light and heat our apartments. If we are unlucky and nobody prepared for the energy transition, we may be cold and huddled beside a single bulb. Depending on how energy policy turned out and how the battles have been going against agricultural pests and diminishing crop returns, we will probably be eating a diet closer to that of 1900 than of 1994: fewer frills and delicacies such as out-of-season greens and fruits from California or Central America. Those who romanticize the idea of a simpler diet have probably not eaten what a lot of people ate, month after month, two or three generations ago: potatoes, corn pone and cabbage; some salt fish or sowbelly. These foods are not very appealing, but they are efficient, energy-wise.

Density means high land prices, which, combined with high lumber prices (check out what plywood costs even now, for example), will have driven housing costs up. Americans will live in a smaller space because of the building and heating costs.

These projections may sound dramatic to the point of flamboyance, but most of the changes described are already under way. It is hard to see how the trend will be reversed in a country growing by 140 million in less than 60 years and another 100 million by 2100.

Statistical and factual analyses like these tend to lose sight of the intangibles. Let us pay them the honor of a paragraph, at least. Nearly a half-century ago in Washington, D.C., one of the delights of spring was to watch and hear the spring migration of the warblers. There is not much to hear, anymore. Extrapolating from Audubon Society bird counts, one can surmise that for each 1,000 Tennessee warblers that came north in 1950, there were only six in 1990. And four of those six will be gone in 2000. A similar lament is due for many species that used to be common: cuckoos, shrikes, orioles, dragonflies. Or, for the children, fireflies. What effect the loss of these insectivores is having on life chains is hard to say. It is certain that something of grace and a source of pleasure is being lost every year, and there is no reason to expect that the trend will turn unless humankind stops commandeering the space that other species once occupied. A larger human population means less room for the others.

In a way, these gloomy projections are optimistic, because they assume that trends will continue as they have been, with no sudden galvanic changes—no turmoil in the Persian Gulf countries or sustained anarchy in our cities; no crop failures or massive new pestilence (the result of our tampering with life systems) affecting crops or people.

Beyond the question of the way we live, there is a more fundamental threat to the survival of life systems.

THE THREAT TO LIFE ITSELF

The impact of human activities on the Earth's life support systems remains to a disturbing degree unknown. Yet already, and with remarkable callousness, we have changed the biosphere so dramatically that other species are disappearing at a rate apparently unmatched since the Cretaceous extinctions. At the worst, we may so alter the planet as to cause the collapse or extinction of our own species. The scientists whom we quoted in chapter 1 were not speaking idly. The ignorant multiplication of chemicals, the massive introduction of nitrogen, sulfur, carbon and phosphorus compounds into the environment, the alteration of the climate, the acidification of soils, the destruction of species with which we are perhaps unknowingly symbiotic—any or all of these problems may be involved in the present wave of extinctions, and some combination of them could possibly imperil the human species.

The third world seems to be headed toward another doubling of population, if their ecologies can bear it, much as they may try to avoid it and despite what we may do to help them. Faced with that prospect, and with the impact it will have on the entire biosphere, what can we in the United States do?

Help to those countries in protecting their resources and environment should be second only to family planning assistance in the priorities for U.S. foreign aid programs. Yet in accordance with the principle that we "think globally, act locally," our primary responsibility lies at home. The national goal should be, first, to avoid adding to the annual load of pollution and environmental degradation; and then, to reduce it.

The population scenario sketched in chapter 2 holds out little hope that we will reach that goal, as a matter of practical politics. With population growth demanding something like an 8 percent increase each decade in food, cars, energy, housing, education and infrastructure, and with the voters demanding that their standard of living be safeguarded at all costs, the nation will not be likely to set aside farms and forests for biological preserves, or stop the proliferation of new chemicals, or lead the way to sustainable farming, or finance an orderly energy transition. As a result, most of the problems we have now are likely to get worse.

What can be done demographically to help assure that these somber projections can be avoided?

4

ALTERNATIVE

DEMOGRAPHIC FUTURES

*This [optimal] balance, in the case of the United States, would
seem to me to have been surpassed when the American population reached, at a very maximum, two hundred million people,
and perhaps a good deal less.*

George Kennan, *Around the Cragged Hill:
A Personal and Political Philosophy*

The demographic challenge facing the American people
is awesome. If there is any hope of coping with the escalating environmental problems of the twenty-first century
through population control, the time to act is now. Any
postponement in making rigorous demographic decisions
will merely exacerbate an already serious problem.

Technological progress must be encouraged to minimize
further damage to the environment and natural resources.
Consumption habits must be drastically altered to bring
them in line with those of other societies, to diminish the
impact of human activity on the environment and to preserve a sustainable natural resource base. Beyond that, the
evidence is clear and convincing: the United States cannot
maintain even a semblance of its current quality of life
without some reduction in population size. The natural
resources available to the nation are not sufficient for ever-
increasing numbers of people. At current levels of consumption, they are not even sufficient for the existing
population. Unless population size is reduced, and as rapidly as possible, the nation's present course will eventually
threaten not only the quality of life but, in the worst-case
scenario, the life support system itself. The challenge is to
reduce population size in a manner appropriate to a democratic society.

REACHING A CONSENSUS ON POPULATION SIZE

Let us begin by assuming that the American people and their political leaders will soon reach an agreement on this all-important issue. Quite an assumption, to be sure! Far too often, people wait until a problem assumes crisis proportions before doing anything about it. We cannot afford that approach with population growth. Postponing a solution just makes things that much worse. The nation must plan for a reduction in population size, and the sooner the better.

That, of course, is easier said than done. First, because of an inherent momentum for growth, numbers will continue to multiply for some time to come irrespective of fertility or immigration reductions. Second, taking that into account, there will be differences of opinion on how much more growth is acceptable before population decline should commence. The faster we try to bring about a turnaround, the more difficult the job will be. Third, while there might be eventual consensus on the need to reduce population size, with so many value judgments involved there is unlikely to be agreement on the optimum eventual size of that population.

The argument for population reduction is not immutable; it is a function of time and place. Just one century ago, many benefits of population growth seemed indisputable. At that time, a robust industrial expansion was taking place and the factories "had a huge appetite for low and semi-skilled labor as America began its glory days as the pre-eminent industrial power."[1] Unskilled workers were needed literally by the millions to fill these new jobs. Furthermore, the nation was actually underpopulated. In 1900, there were some 76 million Americans, mostly in the East. It was an appropriate and ideal time for expansion.

That time is long past, both because of population growth and because the way we live has changed, inflicting environmental damage to a degree undreamed of 100 years ago.

We believe the need for reduction is clear, but how much of a reduction is a more complicated issue. Should the country aim for "less than 100 million," as Cornell University professors David and Marcia Pimentel have suggested?[2] University of Maryland professor Robert Costanza reaches a "prudently pessimistic" estimate of about 85 million at current per capita consumption levels, or twice that with a more energy-efficient "European" style of consumption.[3] The National Science Foundation's Paul J. Werbos concludes that "in the long term, the energy sector and the environment would probably be healthiest if the U.S. population were somewhere around 50 to 100 percent of the present level."[4] Should one of these be our goal as a nation?

Rather than offer detailed responses to these troublesome questions, we are going to take a different approach. To begin, let us set a tentative goal of 150 million Americans by the end of the twenty-first century. This approximates Costanza's suggested maximum population under a "European" life-style. It is also a round number that can be justified in several ways. Specifically, it was the population of the United States after World War II, a time when the country managed to feed its people and support extensive food exports, without the current reliance on commercial fertilizers or artificial pesticides and before it cut down the National Forests and the shelter belts on the Great Plains. The nation was releasing far fewer chemicals into the environment, and it was the principal exporter, not importer, of petroleum products. Although the economic course that led to the present environmental debacle was already embarked upon, there was more space and latitude in which to solve resulting problems than is the case today.

To explore the issue of population goals, we have developed various projections for the twenty-first century. Given the momentum for growth inherent in the population, there is a limit as to how much it can fall in a specific period of time. What is a *reasonable* time table to achieve zero population growth at some level considerably lower than the country's current 255 million?

GETTING THERE

To begin with, it would be pointless to assume that American women will altruistically decide to have but one child for the good of the society. Similarly, ending immigration entirely, while perhaps appealing to some on paper, is equally unrealistic. It is impossible to imagine the United States, this "nation of immigrants," turning away all would-be newcomers, particularly in light of the rapid population growth that will almost certainly continue in the principal sending countries.

Finally, the third demographic variable—mortality—is not open to manipulation for demographic purposes. Deliberate reductions in life expectancy to reduce population growth are, of course, out of the question. Quality of life necessarily includes improved health and increased longevity, even if such progress contributes to population growth. In the projections later in this chapter, it is assumed that life expectancy will rise gradually for all Americans. By 2050, Americans, on average, will expect to live over 80 years, as the Japanese do now.

That said, let us now explore what changes in fertility and immigration *are* within the range of the possible, and how they might be achieved.

FERTILITY REDUCTION

Fertility is the single most important demographic variable. Currently in the United States, women are averaging 2.0 live births according to the most recent statistics on age-specific fertility. As was noted in chapter 2, resident women average about 1.9 births, immigrants about 2.7. How much of a drop in fertility is reasonable in the twenty-first century? The one-child family is out of the question. The lowest fertility rates in recent years in industrialized nations were 1.3 for Italy in 1991 and 1.4 for Sweden in 1985. Sweden's rate has since risen to 2.0, and we expect that the very low rate in Italy is a temporary aberration and will rise soon.

In the United States, the lowest total fertility rate recorded was 1.7 in 1976. The "total fertility rate" (TFR) is a synthetic measure of fertility. It assumes that the age-specific fertility rate of a specific year will hold true throughout a woman's reproductive years. While it is the best measure of fertility available, it can be misleading. For example, the total fertility rate reached 3.7 in 1957, the peak of the baby boom years. Yet data on completed fertility by baby boom mothers indicates that these women never averaged more than 3.2 births over their reproductive years. As Michael Teitelbaum and Jay White put it in *The Fear of Population Decline*, "It is well established in demography that with constant lifetime or cohort fertility, period fertility measures [like the TFR] will increase with change toward earlier timing of childbearing, and decrease with the opposite change of delays in childbearing."[5]

Is it possible for American women eventually to average fewer than 1.7 births? We think it is, but only if an all-out effort is made to achieve such a goal.

Today, fertility varies considerably among subgroups of American women. Rates are highest among the least educated, the poor and among some racial minorities. According to a 1990 survey on the fertility of American women prepared by the Bureau of the Census, Hispanic and Black women have higher fertility than Anglo women. Then again, Hispanics and Blacks are far more likely to be poor and undereducated than Anglos. "Indeed, these structural features explain much of the racial/ethnic differences in fertility in the United States."[6]

Any fertility reduction policy based on race must be totally rejected. Rather, we should examine the reasons for high fertility among certain subgroups of American women and then propose appropriate solutions. As figure 4.1 indicates, the relationship between education and fertility is more significant than that between race and fertility. For example, Anglo women, regardless of years of school completed, have much higher fertility than Black women with a college education.[7] Among women with at least four years

Births per 1,000 Women

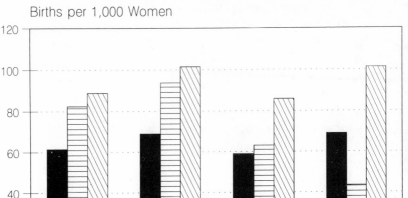

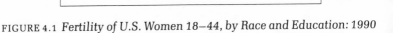

FIGURE 4.1 *Fertility of U.S. Women 18–44, by Race and Education: 1990*

of college, the rate of births per 1,000 women of reproductive age is 43.5 for Blacks compared to 69.1 for Anglos and 101.2 for Hispanics.

The same is true of income. Among families earning more than \$35,000 annually, again, Blacks have *lower* fertility than do Anglos, while Hispanic fertility remains fairly high. There is evidence, however, that Hispanic fertility falls in the second generation and where some assimilation has occurred. As immigrants and their descendants become more proficient in English—a good indicator of acculturation as well as increased education—fertility falls. One study of Mexican-origin women aged 20 to 44 found that those who spoke only English had 2 children on average, versus 3⅓ children for those who spoke no English at all.[8]

Thus, one way to reduce fertility is to increase education and income levels. If the fertility of all subgroups can be brought down to that exhibited by the better educated and the wealthier, irrespective of race, a good start will have been made toward the goal of a total fertility rate below 1.7.

Another factor influencing fertility is female labor force participation. There is a marked relationship between labor force participation and fertility. Working women, especially career women, have lower fertility than those outside the labor force. Thus, improving the opportunities for women in the workplace, through more equitable salary structure and improved child care facilities, for example, will also contribute to reduced fertility.

Nevertheless, improving education, income and work options will not lower fertility enough. Recent data suggest that even the lowest fertility subgroups are averaging 1.8 to 1.9 births, slightly higher than the 1.7 (or less) goal. Census Bureau surveys likewise indicate that women expect to have just over two children.[9] Hence, even those women with relatively low fertility must reduce their fertility even more.

Such a goal can be attained by ensuring that all births are planned and wanted. According to a new study prepared by the National Center for Health Statistics, of the 25.4 million pregnancies that occurred in the United States between 1984 and 1988, an estimated 13.3 million—52 percent—were unplanned.[10] Of these unplanned pregnancies, some were unwanted as well. True "planned parenthood," in addition to encouraging more loving parent-child relations, could definitely bring the fertility rate down to below 1.7.

Better access to effective means of birth control and legal abortion are the best ways to assure that all births are planned. The recent approval by the Food and Drug Administration of Depo-Provera, an efficient contraceptive already in use in several countries, is a step in the right direction. It has delayed endorsement, however, of RU-486, the French abortion pill being tested by the Population Council. This is a relatively inexpensive and safe way to avoid childbirth. Furthermore, it is useful in the treatment of numerous other illnesses, such as Alzheimer's disease.

As for research, the federal government, particularly during the Reagan-Bush years, has generally discouraged the development of new contraceptives, and pharmaceutical industries, fearful of boycotts organized by the far right, have given the issue a wide berth. It is high time that new research on both male and female contraceptives be encouraged by the federal government.

Today, it is estimated that over 80 percent of American women do not have reasonable access to legal abortion facilities. Such a situation is intolerable in a democratic society.

We do not advocate reliance on abortion to reduce fertility. By the same token, women should not have to depend on abortion to ensure that all births are planned and wanted. If reliable contraceptive devices and family planning programs are made available to *all* Americans, adolescents as well as adults, the number of abortions will, we predict, drop drastically. Moreover, sex education should be required of all high school students. The tragedy of teenage pregnancy far outweighs any increase in sexual activity that some claim, probably incorrectly, results from such training.

Even if all these recommendations were followed, though, fertility would not necessarily drop as much as we would like it to. The decision to have or not to have children is made at the couple level. Yet leadership must come from the government. Government policies influence family size decision making partly through the social message they carry. As demographer John Weeks has written,

> Humans are inherently social creatures, not simply rational economic beings, and we are constantly looking about us for clues to social behavior. A consistent set of governmental initiatives aimed at lower fertility is almost certain to have the long-term effect of leading couples to think more consciously about their family size decisions.[11]

It is thus vital that the government develop demographic awareness, encouraging small families in the process.

All proposed legislation, regardless of specific intent, should be evaluated as to its possible impact on fertility, much as the EIS (environmental impact statement) process is now a routine part of decision making in the executive branch. In addition to lowering fertility, this would create an awareness among Americans that population growth is indeed a critical issue.

To be sure, one cannot expect the government to take the lead on such a controversial matter without some encouragement from the people. Yet there is hope that with the end of the Reagan-Bush era, a more enlightened executive will see the advantages of at least limiting, if not stopping, population growth. Certainly, Vice President Al Gore, Jr., both in Congress and through his writings, has expressed a genuine concern for problems associated with population growth.[12] President Bill Clinton has made it clear that abortion rights will be protected and family planning activities expanded. Dr. Joycelyn Elders, the new Surgeon General, also promises to be a strong advocate for family planning, particularly among the nation's youth.

Increased education and income, advances in the workplace for women, improved access to family planning and legal abortion, encouragement from the government—together these can help lower the fertility rate of American women to desirable levels. But it will not be an easy job; the people must be convinced that it is in their best interest, as well as that of the society, to have fewer children.

Fertility Assumptions

If population growth is to end eventually, followed by reductions in size, fertility must be reduced as rapidly as is reasonably possible. We assume in the following projection that the fertility of resident Americans will fall from 2.0 in 1990 to 1.7 in 2000. This is quite a rapid drop in a short period. At the same time, it may be that the current rate is artificially high and that fertility will soon revert to its 1980s level.

We then assume that fertility will continue to drop after 2000, reaching 1.6 in 2025 and 1.5 in 2050. After that, no further declines are anticipated. Again, this would mark a dramatic departure from past fertility behavior. Not only would rates fall to historically low levels; they would also remain low for the entire century. "Two is enough" would have to become a commonplace sentiment accepted by all American families. If all couples refrained from having more than two offspring, the goal of 1.5 births per woman could be reached, since many women have only one child or none.

Such assumptions about future fertility behavior, radical though they are, are attainable if the recommendations put forward above are accepted. Could fertility fall even lower than 1.5? Perhaps, but we doubt that a rate of 1.3 or 1.4 could be maintained. No other country has ever done so for very long. Extremely low fertility would also cause real transitional problems as the proportion of aged in the population rose rapidly.

What about the post-2000 immigrants and their descendants? Their fertility, as we have said, is significantly higher than that of the native-born, approximately 2.7 at present. In addition, this group is constantly being reinforced by new immigrants coming primarily from developing countries where fertility remains quite high.

Optimistically, we posit a scenario in which the fertility of this recent immigrant population falls to 2.5 in 2000 and then drops gradually to 2.0 by 2025 and 1.5 by 2050, with no further change thereafter. If immigration—legal and illegal—remains at one million annually, this goal will be difficult to attain because of the large share of first-generation newcomers in the population. Yet fertility in sending countries may well fall in the twenty-first century. Evidence of declines can already be seen in Mexico and other Latin American countries with strong family planning programs.

South Korea's fertility is actually lower than that of the United States. And more immigrants may come from eastern Europe, where low fertility has long been prevalent. Though optimistic, such assumptions about future fertility among immigrants and their descendants are possible.

The Low Fertility/High Immigration Projection

In the following projection (table 4.1, figure 4.2), based on the fertility scenario just described and immigration maintained at the current level of 1 million annually, the U.S. population will continue to grow for many decades, reaching 337 million in 2050 before starting a very slow numerical decline. Even in 2100, the nation's population will be just under 300 million: 20 percent larger than at present. Throughout most of the twenty-first century, the population will be well above 300 million. So much for reliance solely on fertility reductions—even dramatic ones—to limit population growth! The residents-and-descendants subgroup will peak in 2020 at 291 million, falling to 262 million by 2050, and to 165 million by the end of the century. Between 2050 and 2100, this group will decline in number by almost 100 million.

The post-2000 immigrants-and-descendants subgroup will grow throughout the century despite its gradually declining fertility, thanks to continued immigration. From 13 million in 2010, this subgroup will climb to 74 million by 2050 (22 percent of the total population) and 133 million by 2100 (45 percent of the total).

According to this scenario, the United States of the future will be considerably older than it is today (see table 4.2). By 2050, the 73 million people aged 65 and over will represent almost 22 percent of the population, compared to about 12 percent today. By contrast, children under age 15 will number just under 50 million, making up 15 percent of the population. This is somewhat *less* than the number enumerated in the 1990 census, when that age group comprised about 20 percent of the total population. By 2100, over 26

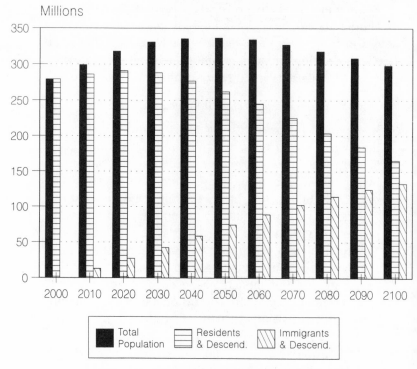

FIGURE 4.2 *Projected Population of the U.S.: 2000–2100*
(low fertility; annual immigration 1 million)

percent of the nation's people will be 65 or over and they
will number 78 million. The number under age 15 will have
fallen to 40 million and will be but 13.5 percent of the total.

IMMIGRATION CONTROL

We have suggested that the U.S. population should fall to
about 150 million within the next century to ensure a sustainable future. Even with drastic, even unprecedented, reductions in fertility, such population goals will not be
approachable as long as nothing is done about immigration.

Some Americans, though concerned about overpopulation, shy away from discussion of reduced levels of immigration. This is true even of certain environmental groups,
including population-control organizations, which focus

TABLE 4.1 *Projected Population of the U.S.: 2000–2100*
(in 000s)
(low fertility; annual immigration 1 million)

Year	Residents and Descendants	Immigrants and Descendants	Total
2000	279,146	NA	279,146
2010	286,075	12,961	299,036
2020	291,003	27,060	318,063
2030	288,366	42,483	330,849
2040	277,104	58,730	335,834
2050	262,361	74,495	336,856
2060	245,394	89,173	334,567
2070	225,057	102,439	327,496
2080	203,799	114,251	318,050
2090	184,203	124,399	308,602
2100	165,414	132,938	298,352

strictly on lower fertility as the key to attaining zero population growth. This reluctance to suggest reductions in immigration is understandable. As a "nation of immigrants," the United States has long been the dreamed-of destination for millions of people from every section of the globe. It is difficult to say "No more" when our own parents and grandparents may have been immigrants. Yet immigration, together with fertility, must be reduced if our population is ever to be limited and eventually cut back to a manageable size.

Then there are those who, concerned solely about immigration, fail to see that fertility remains the main culprit in rapid population growth. The first column in table 2.6 illustrates what would happen if immigration were stopped but nothing were done about fertility: the population would quickly surpass 300 million and remain above that number until late in the next century, falling below it only in 2100. That scenario, the attentive reader will note, is re-

TABLE 4.2 Projected Age Composition of the U.S.: 2000, 2050, 2100
(low fertility; annual immigration 1 million)

Year	Age	Residents and Descendants		Immigrants and Descendants		Total	
		No. (in 000s)	%	No. (in 000s)	%	No. (in 000s)	%
2000	<15	61,095	21.9	NA	NA	61,095	21.9
	15–64	186,353	66.8	NA	NA	186,353	66.8
	65+	31,698	11.3	NA	NA	31,698	11.3
2050	<15	35,132	13.4	14,469	19.4	49,597	14.7
	15–64	161,782	61.7	52,388	70.3	214,170	63.6
	65+	65,446	24.9	7,639	10.3	73,095	21.7
2100	<15	19,991	12.1	20,326	15.3	40,317	13.5
	15–64	94,394	57.1	85,735	64.5	180,129	60.4
	65+	51,029	30.8	26,877	20.2	77,906	26.1

markably similar to the one outlined above, where fertility is lowered but nothing is done about immigration.

A substantial majority of Americans support family planning. On the macro level, having small families helps slow population growth and eases pressures on the environment. On the micro level, parents are better able to provide for one or two children than for four or five. Children from small families are often more likely to be healthy and to succeed in life than those from larger families.

This does not mean that the society or the parents don't love children. Many parents would be happy to have more children, but they know that it is far better to limit themselves to no more than two, for the benefit of both the society and the children.

Family planning and reduced fertility alone cannot solve population growth, however. Bringing up the subject of lower immigration, though, makes one the target of bitter accusations. One is labeled xenophobic, racist or worse. We must keep our perspective. With the quality of life of *all* Americans at stake, it is time to face facts and examine what levels of immigration are appropriate for ending growth and bringing about population decline.

Practical reasons for reducing fertility apply also in the case of limiting immigration, whether the newcomers are from Poland and England, from Mexico and El Salvador, or from Korea and the Philippines. On the macro level, limiting immigration means potentially slower population growth. On the micro level, the society is better equipped to assist fewer immigrants, rather than more, in adapting and progressing in American society; the immigrants themselves then join the American mainstream more quickly, with fewer problems in adjustment.

This does not mean that the society doesn't like immigrants. Immigrants have contributed tremendously to the social and economic success of the United States; they continue to do so today and will in the future. Just as some Americans are "pro-children" but value quality over quantity, so too some are "pro-immigrant" and, again, prefer quality over quantity. This does not make them racists.

It makes no sense to discuss birth control without considering immigration. Both contribute to population growth and must be addressed without fear of emotional attack. If population growth is a problem—as indeed it is—then all sources of population growth must be examined.

IMMIGRATION ASSUMPTIONS AND PROJECTIONS

In 1980, the Select Commission on Immigration and Refugee Policy (SCIRP) recommended that net legal immigration be limited to about 500,000 annually. Ten years later, the Congress passed new legislation *increasing* legal immigration to between 700,000 and 800,000. Little has been done, in the meantime, to reduce illegal entries.

Numerous polls have shown that Americans, being aware of the resource and infrastructure problems facing

TABLE 4.3 Projected Population of the U.S.: 2000–2100
(in 000s)
(low fertility; annual immigration 500,000)

Year	Residents and Descendants	Immigrants and Descendants	Total
2000	279,146	NA	279,146
2010	286,075	7,141	293,216
2020	291,003	14,286	305,289
2030	288,366	22,091	310,457
2040	277,104	30,283	307,387
2050	262,361	38,177	300,538
2060	245,394	45,484	290,878
2070	225,057	52,088	277,145
2080	203,799	57,953	261,752
2090	184,203	62,957	247,160
2100	165,414	67,160	232,574

the nation, favor reduced immigration.[13] Indeed, in a recent
Roper poll, "55 percent of the respondents support[ed] a
temporary moratorium on all legal immigration, except for
spouses and minor children of U.S. citizens."[14] A Newsweek survey from July 1993 arrived at a similar figure, with
60 percent of respondents stating that immigration is "bad
for the country."[15]

We have prepared a projection using the SCIRP recommendation for net immigration of 500,000 per year plus the
low fertility patterns previously described (table 4.3). The
results are not encouraging, given our goal of reaching 150
million as soon as possible.

The population would grow until 2030, when it would
reach 310 million. It would still surpass 300 million at mid-
century, dropping steadily thereafter until hitting about
233 million in 2100—which is still a far cry from 150 million. At this juncture we must ask yet another crucial ques-

tion: Can we, as a nation, enjoy the luxury of waiting so long before attaining our stated goal?

What, then, should be done about immigration? As we have already stated, simply terminating immigration is not a realistic option. While the American public might allow, and even approve, significantly lower levels, an absolute end to immigration would not be acceptable to most people, especially given their own backgrounds. Yet the only projection that comes close to reaching 150 million within the next century assumes just that. Is there a reasonable alternative to no immigration?

Some population-control organizations suggest zero net immigration as a practical goal. That is, as many people would leave the country as would enter it. Because of the massive level of immigration in recent years, the number leaving may well be quite substantial for a few decades. However, eventually such an assumption would require that all the people who come to the United States would later depart! This is clearly unrealistic. In any event, because reliable data are lacking on both emigrants and illegal immigrants, net immigration becomes a problematic standard.

Our proposal is this: first, that annual levels of legal immigration be set at 200,000 beginning in the year 2000; second, that serious efforts be made to put an end to clandestine immigration.

For a decade or two, the number of people leaving the United States may well approximate 200,000 a year, thus offsetting the number entering legally. Thereafter, however, it seems likely that fewer and fewer people—perhaps 20,000 or 30,000 annually—will leave the country.

At the same time, the number entering surreptitiously— about 300,000 a year at present—will be dramatically reduced as the government acts to curb illegal immigration. Yet even with the most aggressive policies, including, for example, an electric barbed wire fence all along the border, eradicating the problem will be very difficult—particularly since many people come legally on tourist visas and then simply stay.

In the final analysis, it seems reasonable to hope that both emigration and illegal immigration could fall over the next century but more or less balance each other in the end. Admittedly, these assumptions are weak, given the paucity of data, but they will have to suffice.

To repeat, this "best bet" scenario assumes that legal immigration will be limited to 200,000 annually. A few more will enter surreptitiously; on the other hand, perhaps as many will leave the country as enter illegally.

At first glance, it might seem that such goals as limiting legal immigrants to 200,000 per year and curtailing illegal immigration are easily attainable, especially when compared to reducing fertility. The nation simply has to adjust its immigration laws.

Nothing could be further from the truth.

Congress is oriented toward *increasing*, not *decreasing*, legal immigration. All recent legislation has been geared to raising levels—witness the 1990 law, which has resulted in immigration gains of perhaps 200,000 annually. It would take a complete turnaround in thinking for Congress to pass new laws *limiting* legal immigration to 200,000 per year. Curiously, polls show that Americans, regardless of background, favor reductions in immigration levels. Indeed, to our knowledge, no American poll has ever found a majority favoring increased levels of immigration. Why, then, does the Congress go against the wishes of the American people?

First, ethnic pressure groups lobby intensively against any attempts to limit immigration. Legislators assume that these organizations speak for their entire constituencies. As the polls suggest, this is far from true.

Second, certain economic determinists and business leaders have convinced many legislators that a labor shortage is imminent and that, even without a shortage, increasing the labor supply is economically advantageous for the country. The *Wall Street Journal* is at the forefront of this movement: "If Washington wants to 'do something' about immigration, we propose a five-word constitutional amendment: There shall be open borders."[16] The fact that the resulting influxes would also result in lower wages is conveniently omitted.

Third, some liberals feel that the nation has a duty to take in the poor surplus populations of depressed areas worldwide. This position is well meant and reflects a concern for humanity, but it fails to consider the overall impact on the nation of these potentially massive numbers of people. It would be far preferable to increase family planning assistance to poorer countries, thus easing their path toward economic development and, in the process, making them more attractive for their own people.

The political tide could be changing, however, propelled by the asylum issue. Under current law, thousands of people who enter the United States illegally can remain and gain legal status by claiming political asylum. Many people, however, use this policy to claim asylum illegitimately and then, as the bureaucratic wheels inch their way around, disappear quietly into the society.

This ploy is especially popular with Chinese illegal immigrants, hundreds of whom showed up recently on a New York City beach. As the *Washington Post* put it, "Experts say specific U.S. policies have turned the ocean between China and New York into a kind of human highway, creating special incentives for Chinese to come illegally and for businesses in New York's Chinatown to support the practice."[17] Particularly relevant to the Chinese situation is a December 1989 Bush administration directive that expanded the definition of political persecution to include anyone adversely affected by a forced family planning policy. If that directive remains on the books, we can expect millions of Chinese to try to enter the United States in the next several years.

Our recommendation of 200,000 arrivals per year would include legitimate refugees and asylum seekers as well as other legal immigrants, with priority given to those who would contribute the most to the society.

Even if the Congress shifted gears and passed new laws

drastically cutting legal immigration, the issue of illegal entry remains. In our projection, we assume that steps will be taken to keep such inflows to a minimum. But again, it will be up to the political powers to act. President Clinton has recommended adding personnel to the Border Patrol; Senator Barbara Boxer (D-CA) has suggested using the National Guard to monitor the border, a proposal that is apparently being considered by the Attorney General. More rigid enforcement of the nation's labor laws and close monitoring of employers who are known habitually to hire illegal immigrants may also help. However, additional deterrents must also be brought to bear. The following, for example, are worth considering: first, proof of legal status or citizenship as a condition for (a) entering into real estate contracts, (b) obtaining drivers' licenses or motor vehicle registrations, (c) qualifying for professional or occupational licensing, (d) enrolling in state or federally assisted colleges, (e) securing business and alcoholic beverage licenses; second, IRS audits of employers found hiring illegal aliens and disqualification of wages paid to unauthorized aliens as deductible business expenses; and third, more expeditious procedures for deportation and summary exclusion of aliens entering illegally.[18] Finally, we must develop a tamper-proof system of identification. Perhaps the health card being proposed for a national health care system, which the Clinton administration insists will be limited to citizens and legal residents, could eventually serve such a purpose. In any event, somehow we must make the United States less attractive for illegal immigrants; this goal, we believe, can be achieved without resorting to draconian measures.

Will these and similar efforts allow the nation to reach a population of 150 million before the end of the twenty-first century?

Table 4.4 and figure 4.3 give us bad news and good news. The bad news is that even with low fertility and very low immigration, the population in 2050 (279 million) will still be 25 million more than it is today, and by the year 2100 it will have just fallen below the 200 million mark. The good

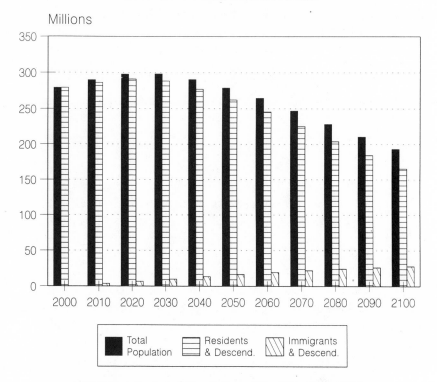

Millions

FIGURE 4.3 *Projected Population of the U.S.: 2000–2100
(low fertility; annual immigration 200,000)*

news is twofold. First, by 2100 the rate of decline will be such that the 150 million goal can be met within another 20 to 30 years. Second, recall that this scenario assumes immigration of 200,000 annually. If the number leaving the country is higher than anticipated and if illegal entries are greatly reduced, net immigration could be lower than 200,000. Say it averaged 100,000 annually; the 2050 population would then be closer to 250 million, while the 2100 population might well be under 180 million.

At that point, we *would* have the luxury of exercising options—to keep moving down, or perhaps to encourage a bit higher fertility or raise immigration levels. It is important to keep in mind that such a scenario in fact creates a momentum for population decline. Increases in fertility or immi-

TABLE 4.4 *Projected Population of the U.S.: 2000–2100*
(in 000s)
(low fertility; annual immigration 200,000)

Year	Residents and Descendants	Immigrants and Descendants	Total
2000	279,146	NA	279,146
2010	286,075	3,648	289,723
2020	291,003	6,624	297,627
2030	288,366	9,856	298,222
2040	277,104	13,215	290,319
2050	262,361	16,384	278,745
2060	245,394	19,270	264,664
2070	225,057	21,878	246,935
2080	203,799	24,176	227,975
2090	184,203	26,095	210,295
2100	165,414	27,697	193,111

gration would eventually be required to avoid any further population loss.

In this scenario, the post-2000 immigrants-and-descendants subgroup will grow throughout the next century, but obviously at a slower pace than if immigration were higher. By 2050, 16 million, or 5.9 percent of the total population, will be either new immigrants or the descendants of post-2000 immigrants. By the turn of the twenty-second century they will number almost 28 million, making up 14.3 percent of the total population.

The combination of low levels of immigration and falling fertility will result in a rapidly aging society (see table 4.5). By 2050, almost one-quarter of all Americans will be 65 or over, while only 13.7 percent will be under 15. By 2100, the respective shares will be 29.4 percent and 12.5 percent. Interestingly, the number of elderly will fall during the second half of the twenty-first century, from 67 to 57 million; the number of children will drop from 38 to 24 million.

TABLE 4.5 *Projected Age Composition of the U.S.: 2000, 2050, 2100*
(low fertility; annual immigration 200,000)

Year	Age	Residents and Descendants		Immigrants and Descendants		Total	
		No. (in 000s)	%	No. (in 000s)	%	No. (in 000s)	%
2000	<15	61,095	21.9	NA	NA	61,095	21.9
	15–64	186,353	66.8	NA	NA	186,353	66.8
	65+	31,698	11.3	NA	NA	31,698	11.3
2050	<15	35,132	13.4	3,128	19.1	38,260	13.7
	15–64	161,782	61.7	11,391	69.5	173,173	62.1
	65+	65,446	24.9	1,864	11.4	67,310	24.2
2100	<15	19,991	12.1	4,202	15.2	24,193	12.5
	15–64	94,394	57.1	17,785	64.2	112,179	58.1
	65+	51,029	30.8	5,710	20.6	56,739	29.4

Although the United States of 2050 and 2100 will be vastly different from that of 1994, the aging of the people should not be viewed with too much apprehension. Throughout this exercise we have kept our definition of "elderly" constant at 65 and over. Yet even today the government has redefined the term: in 2000, the age at which Social Security will be fully available will begin to go up, eventually reaching 67. It may rise even more as time goes on. Furthermore, Americans are living and being productive longer than ever before, and we assume that that trend will continue. Thus, by the middle of the next century, "elderly" may well be defined as 75 and over.

Nor should the relatively small size of the population under 15 concern us too much. Already, as educational levels have risen even higher, it has become more appropriate to think of the "dependent" population as youths aged 0–19.

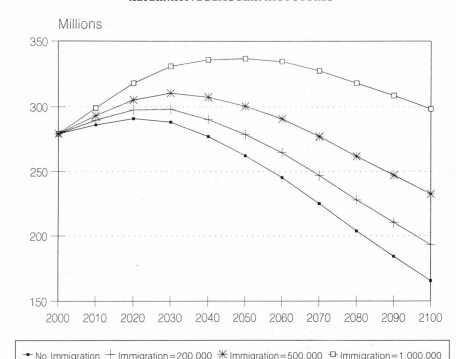

FIGURE 4.4 *Projected Population of the U.S.: 2000–2100*
(all low-fertility scenarios)

That age span, too, may prove to be low by 2050. Bear in mind as well that productivity is no longer a function mainly of the size of the labor force. Indeed, too many untrained people are a major problem for society even now.

CONCLUSION

Our goal of reaching 150 million by 2100 has proven elusive (see figure 4.4 for a summary of the projections). Even with extremely rigid assumptions about low fertility rates and immigration levels, the U.S. population in 2100 will surpass that number by a considerable margin. Perhaps more important is the fact that the population will be close to 300 million by 2030 and remain larger than it is today until about 2065. The population Juggernaut is proving very difficult to slow down, never mind stop entirely.

These projections make one thing abundantly clear: population limitation and eventual reduction cannot occur unless immigration is addressed. While it is of paramount importance that fertility be reduced, that alone cannot accomplish the job.

Some people might consider it sufficient to limit the nation's population to its present size of about 250 million rather than pursuing our more ambitious goal of 150 million. With fertility gradually falling to 1.5 births per woman, the 500,000-immigrants-per-year scenario would allow that level to be reached toward the end of the twenty-first century. Even with this scenario, immigration levels that we currently sustain would have to be cut in half.

Throughout this exercise we have assumed a fertility rate of 1.5. This is extremely optimistic. What if fertility fell to only about 1.7 births per woman, which would still be a historical low? Immigration would then have to be reduced even more if our goals were to be reached in the more distant future.

We have pointed out in earlier chapters that our natural resources and the demands of our infrastructure will not permit the population to stay at the present level for very long without dramatic deterioration of the quality of life. The country needs not stabilization, but a rollback. Yet it would be unrealistic to lay down more restrictive scenarios for future fertility and immigration than those presented in this chapter.

The message is clear: a demographic future compatible with the requirements of the energy transition, the preservation of our farms and forests, clean atmosphere and water supplies, the forestalling of adverse climate change, and the restoration of a decent life for all, including our urban residents, will come about only if we act now. Fertility and immigration must be reduced.

5

THE DIVERGING ROADS

AHEAD

After two years of concentrated effort, we have concluded that, in the long run, no substantial benefits will result from the further growth of the Nation's population, rather that the gradual stabilization of our population would contribute significantly to the Nation's ability to solve its problems.

Letter of transmittal from Chairman John D. Rockefeller III
of the Report of the Commission on Population Growth
and the American Future, to President Nixon,
the Senate and the House, 27 March 1972

Perhaps the most poignant thing about the quotation above is that more than twenty years have passed, the U.S. population has grown by 50 million since then, and not only has nothing been done to address the matter, but no subsequent official U.S. statement of the issue has been as clear and compelling as that report.[1] Because of the national reluctance even to consider the topic, we are allowing the single most fundamental determinant of the nation's future character to be settled by default.

The inaction results from inertia, and from an unwillingness to tackle the explosive issues of fertility and immigration, which must be addressed if the nation's demographic course is to be shaped by anything other than blind chance. The result is a colossal and tragic failure of foresight. We must, at this late date, face the critical question: How do we get the nation to perceive and focus on the hard decision before it?

LAISSEZ-FAIRE OR ACTIVISM?

Let us construct two scenarios, one examining the impacts of continued rapid population growth, the other looking at the impacts of a policy of managed population reduction. The difference between the two populations (table 4.4) starts slowly but mounts with frightening acceleration: from zero in 2000, to 34 million in 2020, 118 million in 2050, and 299 million by 2100—and it is still diverging. The problems don't stop with the passage of time. They get worse.

Can the United States sustain another population doubling? We doubt it, even at far lower standards of living than at present. Nevertheless, such growth is possible. Sad to say, it may even be probable.

We discussed some of the environmental and resource repercussions of unmanaged growth in chapter 3. It may be useful to review those repercussions in light of the "low" series of population projections outlined in chapter 4.

Before we get into the specifics, a few general notes are in order.

First, when pressure is taken off one part of the system, it tends to take the pressure off elsewhere. For example, a reduction in the demand for transportation reduces atmospheric pollution and the release of greenhouse gases; it eases the need for road construction, thus freeing capital for tasks such as the cleanup of toxic dump sites; and it saves foreign exchange that otherwise would have gone to the purchase of oil, thus reducing our balance of payments deficit and so improving the terms of trade. Another example: lowering energy demand saves money and energy, and it lessens pollution by permitting the phasing out of the oldest, most polluting and least efficient power plants.

Second, improvements in one area create opportunities in others. For example, a smaller population requires less food. Less demand for food creates options for action: fertilizer use can be reduced (thereby reducing the pollution of rivers, estuaries and groundwater), or multiple cropping can be substituted for monocultures (thereby reducing the need for pesticides, discouraging the evolution of resistant pests and improving soil conservation), or erosive or poor land can be allowed to revert to rangeland or forest.

Third, and perhaps most important, the object is to seek the optimal solution, not simply to temporize. For example, it is frequently argued that nuclear energy—particularly breeder reactors—can help fill the gap left by the exhaustion of fossil fuels. Yet this assumes that nuclear power is necessary without considering whether it is in fact desirable. Wouldn't the happiest solution be a situation where it was not needed?

Those who would rather not address the population issue look to conservation and technology as the answer. They argue that "you don't need to reduce P (population demand), because we can make sufficient gains in conservation (C) or technology (T) to meet the nation's needs."

There are two flaws in this analysis. First, it does not address what will happen when further gains from conservation become impossible. (If one could sustain 5 percent annual energy savings, by 2050 the nation would be getting by on less than 6 percent of its present energy consumption—an unlikely situation.) Second, it ignores what can be achieved if all three variables—conservation, technology *and* population—are addressed. We will return to this point.

Let us once again make the general observation that all of the population-driven pressures on resources and the environment would be 30 percent less under the managed population scenario than under laissez-faire by 2050, and 60 percent less by 2100. That alone is sufficient argument for the managed population approach.

Having said all that, let us make some particular points about the connection between population reduction and certain pressing problems.

ENVIRONMENTAL DIVIDENDS FROM A SMALLER POPULATION

Energy, Climate and the Atmosphere

Real reductions in population-driven demand will not come quickly enough to satisfy today's pressing problems of air pollution and the energy transition, because the population would not drop below the present level until the 2060s, even under the toughest of our scenarios. Yet by holding P nearly constant, that scenario would allow conservation and technological change to be used to reduce pollution, acid precipitation and the release of greenhouse gases, rather than using up those gains simply to counteract the damage from increased population-driven demand.

The leverage is quite dramatic. To go back to our calculations in chapter 3: under the unrestrained population growth scenario, the annual bill for replacing power plants with less-polluting, new technology is something like $78 billion. This calculation assumes the best present technology. It would substantially reduce present air pollution and acid precipitation, but on a leisurely 40-year schedule, and it would do nothing about climate warming. It assumes no conservation and no movement toward alternative energy, which remains much more expensive than conventional power.

The managed population scenario works out to 0.4 percent annual growth in the first decade, 0.3 percent in the second, no growth from 2020 to 2030, and an accelerating decline thereafter. From 2010 through 2050, the difference between the two population curves amounts to approximately 1 percent annually. This gain could be used to retire old plants on a 30-year cycle rather than every 40 years, or to finance other investment, such as alternative energy technologies. If conservation measures could be put in place each year that saved 5 percent of energy consumption (a modest target in light of the exuberant claims made by proponents of conservation), during the first few years the oldest plants could be retired even faster, on a 12-year cycle. A better alternative would be to use the funds saved to invest in sustainable, non-polluting energy sources, thus addressing the issues of acid precipitation and climate warming as well.

Those savings wouldn't last very long, however. One runs out of conservation measures, and, mathematically, a constant percentage gain gets smaller each year in absolute terms. Nevertheless, the combined gain is impressive, and savings from population decline would kick in as the potential gains from conservation ran down.

These are rough, back-of-envelope computations, but they open up the possibility that real progress can be made, starting now, in controlling the damage humans have caused in climate and the atmosphere. They are very practical arguments for the tough "managed" scenario.

Sludge and Wastes

The problem of waste—toxic sites, leaking petroleum and chemicals tanks, the rising curve of sludge and municipal waste, nuclear waste—is at a crisis point. Contrary to the popular impression, the country is relying more on nuclear power now than ever before; nuclear wastes are accumulating, and the nation faces the problem of how to phase out the aging nuclear plants approaching retirement. Nobody has propounded a technical fix to eliminate the waste stream from nuclear power. The obvious solution is not to need it, which brings us back to the obligation to reduce the population-driven energy demand as soon as possible.

Sewage sludge is a particularly intractable problem. Primary and secondary treatments may reduce the bacterial load, but they do nothing about the nitrates and phosphates in the sludge, and the cost of technologies to deal with them is so astronomical that no government agency has seriously proposed equipping the nation with such facilities. In this instance, population reduction is not just part of the solution; it is, aside from some prospects for substituting sludge for chemical fertilizers (unfortunately, an energy-intensive proposal), substantially the *only* solution.

With toxics and solid wastes, we don't have much choice. We must simply hold on, do what we can afford to do to clean up the identified sites and the new sites that will be discovered as pollutants show up in aquifers or in towns afflicted by mysterious ailments, and try to arrest any further increase in the pollution.

Amid the chorus of demands for more money for health care, long-term care, AIDS and cancer research, job training and education, solid waste management is competing with politically potent spending requirements, and the money simply isn't there. And that points to another advantage of the managed population turnaround: it is close to a no-cost solution. It does not require massive investment in new technologies or the expense of trying to haul more waste farther and bury it deeper. What it requires, indeed, costs very little: a national consensus, some changes in our immigration laws and their enforcement and official encouragement of lower fertility.

Cities and the Forest

Seen more broadly, a population turnaround is of course a "gain/gain" policy, since it saves expense and investment in all those areas categorized above, as well as in infrastructure. Under laissez-faire, maternity hospital beds will be needed for 5.2 million babies in 2050 and 6.1 million in 2100. The figures would be 2.4 and 1.5 million in the population turnaround scenario. Classroom space would be needed for 85 and 95 million in one scenario, and 40 and 26 million in the other. The comparisons could be extended throughout the economy.

Another cost of urban growth is less frequently remarked upon. Cities tend to devour themselves. What was a tree-lined street of single-family homes in one era becomes a parade of high rises or an industrial area when the city has grown. This means a lot of destruction, as well as building. As the demand for building materials, particularly lumber, increases in an era of decreasing per capita availability, the pressure on our forests rises. Moreover, the destruction of the old houses is a waste. As the wood houses in old towns attest, wood can last a lot longer than it is called upon to do in our growing society.

In other words, urban growth adds a multiplier to the demand for wood products in our era of decreasing per capita availability, and thus puts additional pressure upon our forests.

There is also something of an inverse phenomenon. Cities with declining populations, such as Cleveland and Pittsburgh, offer more housing space per capita and more infrastructure such as roads, school buildings and parks. The most rundown part of the housing stock can be removed and perhaps converted to parks and open space. Both these cities had a bad reputation as part of the "rust belt," with industries long departed, but the anticipated unemployment did not occur, in part thanks to population outflow, and the greater sense of openness and habitability strikes anybody who has been there and compared these cities to, say, New York City. Studies of the habitability of cities confirm this impression.[2]

Chemicals

The use of untested or undertested industrial and agricultural chemicals is very close to Russian roulette. Very possibly, even now, we are causing the buildup of toxins that could threaten organisms vital to our own survival. The increased use of chemicals has been driven in large measure by the need for agricultural productivity. If the growth in demand for food can be slowed or stopped, we may be able to take the time to learn more about chemicals before releasing them into the environment.

Agriculture

Farmers will adjust to changed circumstances. Already, the spread of conservation tillage and the recent decline in fertilizer use suggest that they found it unprofitable to use energy and labor on plowing or to pour on chemical fertilizers that did not raise yields. When energy prices go up, that small trend is going to become a ground swell. When pests devour their corn-on-corn cropping, farmers will go back to crop rotations. The farm sector will be in better shape, but yields will probably be down.

The role of demography is to plan ahead for that trend. As the calculations in chapter 1 suggested, we may have a generation or two before the problem of insufficient supply becomes acute, but we must start now if the population Juggernaut is to be stopped by then.

Preserving the Biosystem

A wise nation would be putting aside natural ecosystems much faster than we now are. We could start now with the preservation of all remaining old growth in National Forests and the setting aside of other areas to revert to mature stands. We might, despite local resistance, be able to promote a patchwork of mature riverine and upland stands in the East and South. We have some protected shortgrass rangeland and could protect much more; such an act would be met by bellows of rage from Western senators, but it would have no perceptible effect on the economy. (Protection would not necessarily require the removal of all cattle from the range, but it would undoubtedly require a reduction in their number.) We need comparable protected areas in the Midwestern prairie. Above all, we need to save wetlands from encroachment, draining and contamination.

These things could be done with our present population. It is a matter of will rather than numbers.

The role of demographic planning here is to avoid the kind of population growth that imperils present efforts to save African wildlife. It is hard to protect a principle against hungry people encroaching on wildlife preserves.

In this sense, our ability to head off intensified pressures on agriculture and the forests is central to preserving the sometimes invisible web of the biosphere. So is our success in dealing with the various forms of pollution that have resulted from the industrial revolution and pose threats we do not yet understand to different life forms. Here, as elsewhere in ecological issues, the damage we do is interconnected, and the gains that we make on one front translate into gains on another.

We have attempted to define biodiversity in broader terms than just depletion of wildlife. Humankind should be even more concerned about preserving microorganisms, food chains and existing natural balances. If we can reduce the release of chemicals, the massive use of pesticides and the indiscriminate use of drugs to fight our "subterranean wars," we diminish the threat to that complex web. Those disturbing introductions into the ecosystem arise from the drive for productivity, which itself has been both the product and the prop of the human population explosion. A diminished population would eventually reduce the need for that steady growth in productivity.

With the population turnaround scenario, one can at least dream of a balance a century hence that permits sustainable agriculture, surrounded by extensive woods and natural systems only partly managed for human use, with cities small enough to be civilized, and with our wastes, by-products and contaminants reduced to levels that natural systems, aided by human technology, can successfully buffer.

Perhaps we should take a lesson from the Amish. We might not choose to rebuff new technologies so resolutely as they do, but they know a lot about sustainable management of their little corner of Pennsylvania and could probably teach us a lot.

OTHER BENEFITS OF POPULATION REDUCTION

The advantages of a smaller society go well beyond resources, environment and the infrastructure. Also to be noted are social, economic, cultural and demographic benefits. These become especially apparent if we recall that most of the future growth will come from immigration.

The State of the Cities

Among youthful cities, some growth is good. The following scenario typifies what has occurred over and over again in cities and towns across the nation. Imagine a small town with considerable land area. Every new resident contributes to lowering the cost of providing basic services to all. The more people hooked into the electrical grid, for example, the more people to share its fixed costs. The same applies to police protection, libraries, schools, local roads and so on. These are economies of scale, and reflect "average costs," which is simply the result of dividing the total costs of the service by the total number of users.

In that sense, growth is good: the more people, the less expensive the services. Yet there is a limit to that growth, if it is to be beneficial for all. As the town gets bigger, much of its infrastructure bumps up against its carrying capacity. The original electrical grid no longer suffices; more police must be hired; the town expands and requires a branch library and more personnel; roads and schools no longer satisfy the needs of the growing population. The houses have been built, but now the roads are too narrow, and every expansion generates expensive dislocation. A cloverleaf intersection is orders of magnitude more expensive than a stop light. The result is diseconomies of scale. Rapid growth, instead of lowering the average cost of services, eventually raises it. "Put another way," writes Phillip Longman in *Florida Trend*, "once population growth becomes sufficient to cause diseconomies of scale, marginal cost, which is the cost of providing for one extra person or unit of consumption, begins to rise faster than average costs."[3]

The quality of life of all the citizens then begins to deteriorate. By then, though, they are so convinced of the benefits of growth that they fail to recognize what further escalating costs really mean. Instead they simply adjust to the new demands by installing ever-more services at ever-rising taxes for all. Finally, when they simply cannot keep up, comes the deterioration of services in the big cities, exacerbated by the departure of the better off and more mobile—a situation painfully evident today. The clearest evidence of the truth of this scenario can be found in the difference in tax rates. They are almost invariably higher in cities than in small towns or rural areas.

Unemployment and Social Unrest

Continued rapid population growth complicates efforts to deal with the problems of the nation's underclass. Continued high fertility and massive immigration make it difficult to improve conditions for the nation's indigenous poor and incorporate them into the economic mainstream. Recall the large numbers of young adults who will be entering the labor force in future years, an ever-increasing share of them immigrants. Given current conditions of unemployment, underemployment and a high working-age dropout rate, we are only magnifying the problem by permitting massive immigration.

Figure 5.1 compares the numbers of young people entering the job market under the laissez-faire scenario of chapter 2 with the lowest projection of managed reduction in chapter 4. The graph dramatizes both the accelerating difference between the two scenarios and the problem of demographic momentum. It takes time to turn around. Those young people through 2010 are already born, whether here or in another country. Decisions made now could influence immigration right away, but they will take a generation to affect the native-born cohort entering the job market. Under the high scenario, by the way, the total working-age population will rise rapidly throughout the period; under the low scenario it will fluctuate downward from 2030 on, thus helping to reverse the current tendencies toward rising unemployment and deteriorating wages.

With little prospect of a good job even for the industrious—when hashing at a fast-food restaurant looks like the top of one's realistic career hopes—it is easy to see why young people drift into dependence on welfare and the street society of drugs and crime.

The lower series in figure 5.1 shows what would happen with a managed population turnaround. The young people in that scenario would have a real chance of getting an ed-

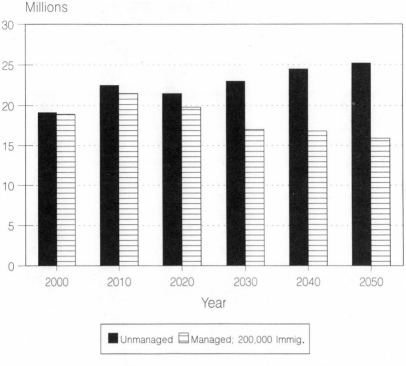

FIGURE 5.1 *Projected U.S. Job-seeking Cohort, Age 20–24*

ucation, and a job. There would be less competition for
entry-level jobs; unskilled workers would then have a better chance to climb the labor ladder and move out of poverty. The motivation to get back into the system rises as
evidence accumulates that the system works and one really
can find a job. Figure 5.1 should also remind us that if we
had listened to the Rockefeller Commission in 1972, we
could have been over that 2010 hump by now.

The national tendency has been to associate the dropout
problem strictly with the unskilled and poor. This may no
longer be valid. The technological revolution and foreign
competition are moving the problem into the middle class,
where even skills in management, computers, electronics
or high-tech construction cannot protect against sudden
joblessness. The layoffs at Boeing, General Electric, IBM,

and other leading companies demonstrate a corollary to the Carter/Leontief thesis that productivity in a modern economy is a function more of capital and technology than of the number of workers. Since wealth and productivity rest in a small fraction of the population, redistributing income poses a major social problem.

This conundrum must be dealt with. A shrinkage of the labor pool would ease that social problem, even as a smaller population would improve the chances of dealing successfully with environmental and resource problems.

These social problems are becoming critically important. They could destroy our society.

Economics

The United States is moving toward a two-tiered society, with a few people enjoying unparalleled prosperity and many more stuck in poverty and low-paying jobs. With so many people available for the unskilled work, there is little incentive to modernize industries and farms to compete internationally in the twenty-first century. High fertility and immigration retard the modernization of American industry. They encourage American business to rely on cheap labor rather than technological improvements. As long as millions of poorly educated young people keep entering the labor force, little hope exists for overall economic improvement.

President Clinton has made it clear that education is the key to an improved economy in a high-tech era. Secretary of Labor Robert Reich echoes that thought:

> A work force possessing a good basic education, which can efficiently bring the fruits of its labors to the global economy, can attract global capital for its performance of moderately complex tasks. . . . But without adequate skills . . . the relationship can be the opposite—a vicious circle in which global money and technology are lured only by low wages and low taxes. . . . Theoretically, it can continue to push wages downward until the citizens

of the nation have a standard of living like that typical of the Third World.[4]

Under present conditions, the young adult population will grow significantly throughout the first half of the next century, largely because of immigration. If this situation endures, hope for improved educational levels in the work force at large seems dim.

The Preservation of Space

Population growth, as we have seen, has a deleterious effect on the environment and leads to resource overutilization. But even if, through some miracle of twenty-first-century science and technology, solutions could be found for all the problems we have examined, 400 million Americans would still pose enormous problems for the society. For example, national parks will probably not increase in either number or size, but the number of visitors could double. It is no consolation to say that future energy and transportation constraints may limit the pressures on parks; in that case the people will simply be stuck in the cities.

With 150 million more people than at present, how many more airports would be needed, and tolerated, and at what distances from urban centers? Would the skies over a nation of 400 million people be as "friendly" as they are today? And what will these urban centers look like?

It is difficult to imagine a more central subject for federal concern than how and where Americans will live in the decades and centuries to come. The dynamics of our existing urban configurations have generated a momentum which is likely to produce more of the same in the future unless a systematic effort is launched to create new opportunities for the 50 million new Americans who will have to find a home within the next two decades.

These words, written in 1971, are taken from a *Population Bulletin* entitled "Where Will the Next 50 Million

Americans Live?"[5] Now we must ask: Where will the next 150 million Americans live?

The additional 150 million people will not be distributed randomly throughout the nation. California's population, for example, will probably surpass 50 million—19 million more than in 1993. Florida and Texas could each reach 30 million. The nation's metropolitan areas will be crowded beyond our wildest imaginings. A Los Angeles or New York with 20 to 25 million inhabitants is certainly within the realm of possibility.

The nation's suburbs can be expected to expand ever farther from the central cities, unless stopped by energy scarcities. Neither prospect is particularly attractive. We will see more and more sprawl; more and more unsightly shopping centers; more and more automobiles, further worsening the nation's air-pollution problems. Either that or the same populations will be cooped up more tightly in existing settled areas.

Faced with the myriad problems caused by population growth, one is tempted to ask why anyone would favor an expansion of the American population.

THE HINDRANCES TO A POPULATION POLICY

The Seductive Quality of Growth

There is a certain seductive quality to growth, whether in individuals, in cities, in states or in nations. "Tall" is generally considered to be favorable; "short" less so.

The media also worship at the Holy Grail of growth. For example, on the popular TV game show "Jeopardy," college-level contestants were asked which country would surpass China in population within the next century. Two of the three accurately identified India. The third replied, "The United States." Such an answer from a Harvard student was surprising. Even more surprising was the comment of the host, Alex Trebek: "That is a noble thought, but unfortunately it is incorrect."

Alex Trebek is an intelligent individual. His comment on

"Jeopardy" was made on the spur of the moment, and no doubt he does not favor a U.S. population of over one billion people! Yet this is but one more example of how the American public has been led to believe that growth is good. We have forgotten E. P. Schumacher's wise sentiment that "small is beautiful." Rather, we have been persuaded, and were so particularly in the Reagan era, that "growth is good."

Cities proudly proclaim that they have surpassed a neighboring metropolis in population. An Orlando economist noted with glee that Orlando's "population growth still ranks with the strongest in the nation and . . . continues to close the population gap on Tampa and Miami."[6] Meanwhile, the news that San Jose had surpassed San Francisco in population during the 1980s was met by the latter city with dismay.

The injunction "Be fruitful and multiply" has a very strong hold on the American mind. Not only do Americans have a love affair with growth; they fear an end to growth. Our prestigious business schools, from Harvard to Stanford, teach how to adjust to population growth, not population decline. Demographer Lincoln Day, in the *Population Bulletin*, puts it this way:

> What is feared about zero growth has less to do with the consequences of this rate of growth itself than with the consequences of moving too rapidly onto unfamiliar demographic ground before social attitudes and institutions have had the chance to adjust to the new demand posed.[7]

The wisdom of George Kennan provides a refreshing commentary:

> I can think of no place in the Western world or in other regions where population *ought* to be growing. If the preservation of this planet as a suitable habitat for civilization is the overriding imperative of our time, and if population growth is itself the greatest threat we face to the intactness of that habitat, then why should we wish to see further growth of this nature?[8]

Fortunately, the United States can look to both the West and the East to observe societies that have exhibited little growth over the past few decades and have adjusted well to the changing circumstances. Between 1982 and 1992, the combined populations of the United Kingdom, France, Germany and Italy grew from 363.2 million to 377.7 million, representing a scant average annual growth rate of 0.32 percent. Japan's population rose from 124.4 million to 128.5 million, an average annual rate of just over 0.4 percent. Given the age composition and the low fertility in these countries, population decline there can be expected soon. The demographic experience of these countries, moreover, suggests that population growth is not a sine qua non for economic success.

The Psychology of Denial

The conjecture is hard to prove, but there seems to be an unconscious element of denial involved in the nation's general reluctance to deal with population. As an abstraction, the idea of stopping population growth became popular in the 1960s and early 1970s, but when the reality sank in that deliberate population change can come about only by consciously changing immigration and fertility patterns, the idea lost favor. A generation brought up to oppose prejudice sees xenophobia in any effort to restrict immigration, racism in any move to lower fertility. Few people are aware that fertility is a function more of education and income than of race.

On another front, right-to-lifers associate family planning with abortion. There is no necessary reason why fertility reductions cannot be achieved without abortion, but in practice so far they have tended to go together, and the association has stuck in the public mind. In fact, the 1972 Rockefeller Commission report (see chapter 2) was summarily brushed aside by President Nixon, despite his own views "in favor of" population limitation, because it advocated increased access to abortion as a way of stopping population growth—an unpopular position in an election year.

Painful as it may be, immigration and fertility are the two accessible variables in population growth. The point is hard to miss. Therefore, the easiest way to avoid facing the painful issues at hand is simply to deny there is a population problem at all.

The opposition to limiting immigration and fertility comes in large part from people of good will who believe their position to be the moral one. Yet moral goods sometimes conflict. If unrestrained population growth leads to the results sketched out in this book, Americans are going to see some cherished ideals eroded away. We need to recognize that unrestricted immigration pits a benefit to the stranger (however deserving) against the well-being of our own poor and disenfranchised and risks passing on a more impoverished country to our descendants. To oppose limiting fertility is to favor the birth of unwanted children, many born in situations where they almost certainly cannot flourish. To be morally consistent, the opponent of abortion should be the proponent of birth control.

One can hardly be confident that a revolution in thinking will occur before population growth itself makes the choices painfully apparent and we have lost the opportunity to anticipate change rather than simply react to it.

The Suspicion of Big Government

Government, apparently, is not getting any more popular as growth forces it increasingly to intrude in the private affairs of the citizenry. This animosity is compounded by the facile observation that "government can't do anything right." The prevailing mindset holds out little hope that the government will be able to lead a shift of national policy toward limiting population growth. That would be social engineering on an almost unprecedented scale, in a country traditionally suspicious of governmental direction.

The most hopeful precedent was the nation's willingness to follow President Franklin Delano Roosevelt in 1933, a time marked by a severe crisis of confidence. The problem with that parallel is that demography grinds slowly, even if it grinds fine. We are not presently dealing with a perceived crisis, and it is more difficult to mobilize an appropriate sense of urgency.

One solution is for the ideas to come from people who are seen as leaders but not necessarily as "government," such as George Kennan, widely recognized as a wise elder states-man. The problem is that the occasional voice of such per-sons is unlikely to be heard when decisions are made on issues such as immigration policy, welfare or tax laws, which in the real world create the conditions that encour-age or discourage population growth. Clearly, some lasting mechanism is needed to mobilize such advice when it will influence those decisions. We will return to that thought at the close of this chapter.

The Pursuit of Self-Interest

It is hardly novel to observe that public interest conflicts with self-interest in the narrow sense. Even people who un-derstand the social and environmental damage that results from further population growth may espouse it in matters of personal convenience—prosperous people who want cheap domestic help, for instance, or businessmen who want cheap labor, or ethnic politicians hoping for a larger constituency, or perhaps even educators who benefit from larger school-age cohorts.

Advocacy for population limitation must be sufficient to overcome the opposition, some of it very tenaciously held, to any deliberate action to influence demographic change. We have pointed out how population growth is contribut-ing to social malaise, environmental deterioration and the overutilization of resources, as well as placing an increas-ing burden on the nation's infrastructure. The evidence is overwhelming: with present consumption patterns the na-tion's population has already exceeded its carrying capac-ity, and as a result the quality of life of most Americans is deteriorating. Yet the seductive charm of population growth remains strong; the pursuit of self-interest is biased against a broad view. Rather than face up to the consequences, people tend simply to continue trying to adjust to population growth, regardless of the costs. It is time that we decide which direction to follow: a laissez-faire policy and population approaching 500 million by 2100, or a managed approach that could lead to a population dropping below 193 million by that time.

THE CHALLENGE OF POPULATION REDUCTION

The arguments for population reduction are strong, but resistance to taking practical action is perhaps stronger. Can we even hope that people will see the light, or must we simply acquiesce to letting the population Juggernaut roll on?

In principle, the question should answer itself: if a smaller nation would be a better nation, persons of good will should be trying to bring it about, whatever the odds. On a more practical level, some fundamental changes of thinking must occur if there is to be any chance for success.

The Human Place in the Universe

In a brief passage of considerable beauty, the Rockefeller Commission report said,

> It is comfortable to believe that changes in values or in the political system are unnecessary, and that measures such as population education and better fertility control information and services will solve our population problem. They will not, however, for such solutions do not go to the heart of man's relationship with nature, himself, and society. According to this view, nothing less than a different set of values toward nature, the transcendence of a laissez-faire market system, a redefinition of human identity in terms other than consumerism, and a radical change if not abandonment of the growth ethic, will suffice. A new vision is needed—a vision that recognizes man's unity with nature, that transcends a simple economic definition of man's identity, and that seeks to promote the realization of the highest potential of our individual identity.[9]

We are glad the Rockefeller Commission said that; we might not have had the temerity.

The people will have to change their thinking about growth, about the economy, about consumption. Albert Einstein, in a slightly different context, warned: "We shall require a substantially new manner of thinking if mankind is to survive."[10] Americans will require a new mode of thinking if they are to stop the population Juggernaut.

Our hopes would probably vanish if we believed that all Americans would have to change their views for a population growth turnaround to succeed. Such a change of thinking must, however, occur among the opinion makers of the nation. We need to reconcile the concern for humanity with the broader concern for the system that supports us if the nation is to make the sacrifice necessary to repair the damage already done, to avoid further damage and to foster the preservation of an ecosystem that is not just a reflection of ourselves.

The Role of the Poor

It may be too much to expect such abstractions to appeal to the presently disenfranchised. To people concerned first and foremost with their own immediate survival, these are distant ideas. To those who have lost hope and self-respect, the future may seem irrelevant. Without their cooperation, however, there will be little prospect of a population turnaround, because immigration and fertility tend to be highest among the poor and uneducated.

The point to be made to such people is that reductions in immigration and fertility would help them first of all. The rest of society would then benefit as their problems are addressed and they are brought into the mainstream. In fact, they probably understand their own self-interest far better than we think. It is worth noting that, although some self-proclaimed Hispanic leaders oppose immigration restrictions, opinion polls invariably show that the people are ahead of them: solid majorities, among minority groups as well as non-Hispanic Whites, believe there are too many immigrants.[11]

An education campaign is needed, led by people the disenfranchised trust, to explain how lower fertility would benefit them and their children. Think of the money now allotted to welfare, including AFDC, and spent futilely on efforts to control lawlessness and drugs. If that effort could be concentrated on nurturing a smaller number of people and helping them to compete for good jobs, we might begin to see a reversal of the alienation and hopelessness that now mark our inner cities.

E Pluribus Unum

On the individual level, the people have to understand the long-term goal and press their leaders to pursue it. They, hopefully encouraged by their governmental leaders, must willingly limit their families to two offspring *for the benefit of the society*. They must also take the lead in demanding immigration legislation that limits entries in a fair and humane way—again, *for the benefit of the society*. On the social level, it must become fashionable for a city or state to be "smaller" than the "bigger" neighbor. This is already happening to a certain extent: Oregon and Vermont come to mind.

If these goals are to be realized, a strong sense of community must emerge, something that is disturbingly missing today as multiculturalism comes to the fore, elbowing out the mutual adaptation appropriate for the twenty-first century. Unfortunately, extreme multiculturalism argues for the primacy of the language and culture of one's genetic and historical roots. It gives rise, Arthur Schlesinger, Jr., charges,

> to the conception of the U.S. as a nation composed not of individuals making their own choices but of inviolable ethnic and racial groups. It rejects the historic American goals of assimilation and integration. And, in an excess of zeal, well-intentioned people seek to transform our system of education from a means of creating "one people" into a means of promoting, celebrating and perpetuating separate ethnic origins and identities. The balance is shifting from unum to pluribus.[12]

145

Total assimilation, however, means a loss of identity for the many groups that make up the United States. It is a demographic fact that the nation will become increasingly diverse, irrespective of fertility or immigration levels. Thus, any attempt to achieve the complete assimilation of all Americans of various ethnic and racial backgrounds into what has been called "Anglo conformity" will fail abysmally, and deservedly so. Diversity should be welcomed as it has been in the past, but only providing we remember our national motto: Out of many, one.

The challenge to the United States, then, is to ensure that all its residents, of whatever background, have equal access to all avenues to success. While they deserve the option of maintaining their own subculture within the broader society, they must adapt to the mainstream culture, at the same time contributing to that culture's ever changing content. As the nation becomes increasingly multi-ethnic, it is important that it choose a form of adaptation that combines the best of pluralism and assimilation. As columnist Pat Truly has written, "We are destined to be diverse, divided by race and age and income and musical taste and religion and political philosophy and language and you name it. Yet all that would matter less if only we were also agreed on some common purpose."[13]

The Need for Community

Only if Americans accept some form of adaptation that takes the best from both cultural pluralism and cultural assimilation can a sense of community ever emerge. Ours is a nation that historically has emphasized national identity over ethnicity, yet at present we are met by an obsessive preoccupation with ethnicity, and doubts about our true identity abound.

> At the back of these doubts is the most haunting question of all: whether, as is affirmed in the American civil religion, national allegiance can be, wholly or primarily, a matter of subscription to a set of abstract principles. This tenet is, like nationalism itself, one of the constitutive fea-

tures of modernity and its humanist religion of the Enlightenment. The question is whether it may turn out to be simply one of the illusions of modernity.[14]

It is our belief that the set of abstract principles that has long guided the United States can be accepted by its increasingly diverse people if some sense of community emerges—specifically, a sense of national community, where awareness of group identity embraces concern for all the members of the group, even if that group's population is 250 million. Without that glue of a sense of community, individuals will see themselves as belonging to subgroups. They will be unwilling to pursue demographic goals that need the cooperation of all citizens, even if they understand those goals, unless they see them as benefiting themselves. They will, for instance, resist implementing lower fertility if they see it as reducing their own group's power vis-à-vis competitive groups.

In *The Structure of Scientific Revolutions*, Thomas S. Kuhn described how guiding paradigms change over time. People go for years believing one thing—that the Earth is flat, or that the sun revolves around the Earth—despite mounting evidence to the contrary. Suddenly they realize the magnitude of the conflicting evidence, change their minds and wonder why they ever believed otherwise.

It is time for a major paradigm shift in our way of thinking.

It is time to move toward a more communitarian mode of social interaction. In the words of the sociologist Amitai Etzioni,

> The 1980s [and many decades prior] was a decade in which "I" was writ large, in which the celebration of the self was a virtue. Now is the time to push back the pendulum. The times call for an age of reconstruction, in which we put a new emphasis on "we," on values we share, on the spirit of community.[15]

Rights must be balanced with responsibilities.

To facilitate this, Americans probably need a dose of

what the philosopher Michael Lerner has called "the politics of meaning," which "seeks to level the playing field by creating economic, political, and social incentives for social and *ecological* responsibility"[16] (emphasis added). Again, rights must be balanced with responsibilities.

If we, as a society, can move in this direction, a major demographic paradigm shift would follow logically. We must cease thinking of population growth as being intrinsically good; we must accept the fact that population growth must end, and the sooner the better.

CONCLUSION

A formidable list of conditions must be achieved if the country is actively to shape its population future. However, if the odds are not very good, the stakes are high.

The knowledgeable proponents of a focused population policy are divided and ineffective. Particularly in the academic community, where much of the knowledge lies, one regularly encounters a sort of gentlemanly aversion to overt advocacy. Advocacy groups are small and scattered, and even those environmental organizations that recognize the costs of continued population growth are paralyzed by the fear of being labeled xenophobic or racist. They therefore limit their advocacy to generalizations and are silent when the real issues—such as the 1990 Congressional debate about increasing immigration quotas—arise.

They need to be reassured: American public opinion, as we have noted, is not as hung up on the immigration issue as they seem to imagine. Moreover, they need to form an effective coalition to assure they are heard—much as General William Draper and the Population Crisis Committee did on the world population issue over a generation ago.

The government needs a systematic process for examining the lateral and long-term impacts of present trends and proposed policies. Such a process would identify the impacts and connections of the sort described in this book. It would help to bring population into national decision making. This process is called "foresight." After the *Global 2000*

Report to the President in 1980, there was widespread enthusiasm among environmental and population groups for a better foresight process, and most of the major environmental groups in the country remain officially committed to it. But the idea languished during the Reagan and Bush administrations.[17] Vice President Gore should be an active proponent. As a congressman and then senator, he introduced successive proposals for a "Critical Trends Assessment Act" to improve the government's capacity to identify important trends and to forewarn it of the consequences of proposed policies. Passage of that bill alone would be an important step toward including population in national decision making.[18]

Various opportunities will present themselves for mobilizing a debate on population growth. The most immediate is perhaps the U.N. International Conference on Population and Development scheduled for fall 1994. Other opportunities will follow.

The 1980 *Global 2000 Report to the President* was the most ambitious governmental effort to bring population, resource and environmental issues together since the Rockefeller Commission report (though, partly from awareness of the fate of the earlier report, it was less forthright about population impacts).[19] The report was followed, in one of the last acts of the Carter administration, by a now almost forgotten book of policy recommendations, *Global Future: Time to Act.* Among the proposals was "a national population policy which addresses the issues of: population stabilization; availability of family planning programs; . . . [and] just, consistent, and workable immigration laws."[20] The present administration might be persuaded that a similar survey is due, one mobilizing private scholars as well as government specialists. We would be fortunate if it came out with recommendations as strong as those of 1981.

Such activities would, with luck, inspire a reinvigorated private effort to keep a spotlight on population and the demographic impacts of proposed national policies. We must bring the population issue to center stage. If the government does not take the initiative, perhaps the best way to mobilize a critical mass would be to convene a national conference that explores these vexing issues that face all Americans and that may change the course of the nation in the twenty-first century.

In any event, the topic should not remain in official limbo. Amid the short-term preoccupations of government, and with all the long-term problems facing the nation, there is no single issue so fundamental, or so deeply intertwined with other issues, as the scale and direction of population change.

APPENDIX

THE DEMOGRAPHIC ASSUMPTIONS

Preparing population projections requires, most importantly, making assumptions about future demographic behavior, be it fertility, mortality or migration. In this appendix we examine each demographic variable to note current trends and extrapolate a possible future. These are in no way predictions; they simply illustrate what might happen *if current trends* persist through the next century.

Fertility

The "baby bust," which began in the early 1970s, has apparently come to an end. By 1990, women were averaging more than two births. For most of the 1970s and 1980s, the total fertility rate was about 1.8. During the four-year period 1986–1989 it rose from 1.84 to 2.01, and births topped 4 million for the first time since 1964. Part of this increase is due to delayed childbearing. More American women are working in career-oriented jobs, marrying later and so putting off having children until over age 30. These over-30-year-olds are themselves part of the baby boom cohort; thus fertility has risen temporarily. At the same time, birth rates have also increased among women under 30, presaging a possible increase in completed family size.

Differential fertility among ethnic groups is another significant variable. Recent data from California show that fertility rates among Asians and Hispanics have been climbing since 1987. Such increases might be partially explained by "shifting shares," as we suggested earlier. Study after study has shown that minority fertility is likely to fall in the second and third generations. However, because of consistently high levels of immigration, first-generation immigrants remain numerous. If high levels of immigration persist, declines in overall minority fertility may not be forthcoming because of the "shifting shares" within that population. The relative share of the first generation, exhibiting higher fertility, remains large compared to those of the second and third generations, who presumably have lower fertility. Thus, it is entirely possible that fertility levels among minorities may not fall as rapidly as generally expected.

Nevertheless, it seems unlikely that overall American fertility will continue to climb, given the influence of the women's movement and a growing reliance on contraceptives, including newly approved methods like Depo-Provera, and legal abortion to limit family size.

Given all these caveats, we assume that for the resident population (which will be increasingly diverse in ethnic composition), fertility will stay at about 2.0. The fertility of twenty-first-century immigrants will likely be higher, especially if immigration from Latin America remains large. Hispanic fertility in the United States approximates 2.8, with Asian rates being considerably lower. Fertility data are not available by group for the foreign-born. The data simply reflect the fertility of all persons of various ethnic backgrounds, regardless of place of birth. The fertility of the foreign-born is undoubtedly higher than that of the second and third generations.

We assume, therefore, that for the post-2000 immigrants and their descendants, irrespective of ancestry, fertility will be 2.7 at the onset of the century and will fall gradually to 2.3 by 2050 and 2.0 by the end of the century. The drop reflects the fact that over time an increasingly larger share of that population will be native-born and thus should have lower fertility. It also takes into account the fact that fertility in countries of origin is also expected to drop in future years.

Mortality

Life expectancy is now at its highest level in American history: 72 years at birth for males and 79 years for females. Progress has been noted throughout the twentieth century, and we expect to see further gains over the next hundred years, though at a somewhat slower pace than in the recent past.

For residents and immigrants alike, we assume that life expectancy will reach 78 for males and 85 for females by 2050 and remain constant thereafter. (In comparison, the people of Japan, the longest-lived in the world, now have a life expectancy of 76 and 82 for males and females respectively.) In the United States, a changing ethnic composition may retard progress as minorities, with their lower life expectancies, become a larger share of the population. In addition, the impact of AIDS as well as environmental decay may delay life expectancy improvements in future years.

Immigration

Although future immigration is far more difficult to estimate than either fertility or mortality, it is probably the most important variable in our projections.

International movements depend on many imponderables such as the economy and political stability of the sending countries as well as the economic condition and legislative mood of the receiving country. On the one hand, political disturbances in Latin America or Asia could result in massive refugee movements toward California and Florida; on the other, future acts of Congress could change immigration levels, as occurred in 1990. The General Accounting Office projects an increase of about 200,000 in annual legal immigration over the pre-1990 figure of 500,000.

Legal immigration is assumed to increase given the 1990 legislation. But determining that level today is not easy. Two other movements contribute to net immigration as well: illegal immigration and emigration. Estimating with any assurance how many people will enter the country illegally is difficult. Nor is the number of people who leave the United States in any given year known precisely, as the INS long ago stopped keeping such records. Even less information is available on how many illegal immigrants are sojourners, returning to their native land whenever the economy allows.

Given all these uncertainties, net immigration into the United States can be estimated only with educated guesses. The most recent Census Bureau projections assume the number will remain constant at 880,000 annually. The demographers John Long and D. B. McMillen, analyzing Census Bureau statistics and critiquing the bureau's 1989 projections, estimate that actual levels of illegal immigration may have been such that total net immigration is closer to 750,000. Another study has calculated that legal immigration *alone* may reach 900,000 by 1995. These two estimates were based on the pre-1990 law. Given the changes instituted with that legislation, as well as untold thousands of illegal entries, we feel that, even with emigration, the average net immigration into the United States will approach 1 million for the near future. This number approximates current trends in international migration and is similar to the assumption used in the Urban Institute study (see chapter 2). It may, however, be driven upward as individuals amnestied under the 1986 legislation continue to gain citizenship and petition for the legal entrance of relatives.

NOTES

INTRODUCTION

1. For a fuller treatment, see also Lindsey Grant and John Tanton, "Immigration and the American Conscience," in *Progress as if Survival Mattered* (San Francisco: Friends of the Earth, 1981); and Lindsey Grant, *The Timid Crusade* (Teaneck, N.J.: Negative Population Growth, Inc., 1994).

2. The quotation is from Pope John Paul II's address in Kaunas, Lithuania; Associated Press, 6 September 1993.

3. Thomas J. Espenshade, Leon F. Bouvier and Brian Arthur, "Immigration and the Stable Model," *Demography* 1, no. 19 (1982): 130.

4. Al Gore, *Earth in the Balance: Ecology and the Human Spirit* (Boston: Houghton Mifflin, 1992), 240.

5. See, for instance, Lindsey Grant, *A Population Focus for U.S. Aid* (Teaneck, N.J.: Negative Population Growth, Inc., NPG Forum Series, June 1987). Partly because of pressure from population and environmental organizations, population funding is rising sharply in the new Congress, but it has yet to be given the priority it deserves.

6. Latino National Political Survey, sponsored by the Ford, Rockefeller, Spence and Tinker Foundations, released 15 September 1992, table 7.23. It is somewhat ironic that one of the sponsors, the Ford Foundation, is a principal source of financial support to at least one Hispanic "leadership" group that advocates increased immigration.

CHAPTER 1

1. A National Research Council sample study found that test data permitted a complete health assessment of 18 percent of drugs, 10 percent of pesticides, 5 percent of food additives, 2 percent of cosmetics and none of the other chemicals in commerce. World Resources Institute (WRI), *World Resources, 1987* (New York: Basic Books, 1987), fig. 13.1, p. 204.

2. "Population Growth, Resource Consumption and a Sustainable World," news release by the National Research Council (NRC), Washington, D.C., 26 February 1992.

3. Daniel E. Koshland, Jr., "For Whom the Bell Tolls," *Science*, 16 September 1988, 1405. (Reprinted by permission of *Science* magazine, copyright 1988 by the AAAS.)

4. WRI, U.N. Environmental Program (UNEP) and U.N. Development Program (UNDP), *World Resources, 1992–93* (New York: Oxford University Press, 1992), 200.

5. See, for example, Stephen E. Tennenbaum and Robert Costanza, "The Plight of the Chesapeake," in *Elephants in the Volkswagen*, edited by Lindsey Grant (New York: W. H. Freeman, 1992), chap. 8.

6. Environmental Protection Agency, *National Priorities List Fact Book*, February 1991.

7. Council on Environmental Quality, *U.S.A. National Report* (Washington, D.C.: CEQ, 1992), 332. See also discussion by the Natural Resources Defense Council and the National Solid Wastes Management Association, cited in the *New York Times*, 23 October 1988, 4F.

8. Robert McConnell, "Population Growth and Environmental Quality in California: An American Laboratory," *Population and Environment*, September 1992, 17.

9. WRI, UNEP and UNDP, *World Resources, 1990–91* (New York: Oxford University Press, 1990), 324.

10. *Statistical Abstract of the U.S.*, 1962, 1992.

11. Leon F. Bouvier and Bob Weller, *Florida in the 21st Century: The Challenge of Population Growth* (Washington, D.C.: Center for Immigration Studies, 1992), 164.

12. In December 1990, 2.968 million youth aged 16–24 had no work and were not in school. The "employed" figure includes those with part-time jobs. From Bureau of Labor Statistics, *Employment and Earnings*, January 1991, tables A-1 and A-4.

13. This discussion and graph are drawn from Lindsey Grant, "The L.A. Riots and U.S. Population Nonpolicy," paper prepared for Negative Population Growth, Inc., NPG Footnote, May 1992.

14. See note 12.

15. David Pimentel and Marcia Pimentel, "Land, Energy and Water: The Constraints Governing Ideal U.S. Population Size," in Grant, ed., *Elephants in the Volkswagen*, 19.

16. U.S. Geological Survey, *Estimates of Undiscovered Conventional Oil and Gas Resources in the United States—A Part of the Nation's Energy Endowment* (Washington, D.C.: U.S. Government Printing Office, 1989). The estimate was reaffirmed in 1991 (*Science*, 12 July 1991, 146–152); it was corroborated by a large panel of academic and oil company geologists; it represents recoverable reserves at current technology and price levels, but the anticipated price elasticity of supply was very low.

17. Preliminary estimate from U.S. Department of Energy, Energy Information Administration, *Short Term Energy Outlook, Third Quarter 1993.*

18. Data on replenishment rates and acreage from Burlington Resources, Inc., Seattle, third quarter report 1992. The acreage comparison is for 1985 and 1991.

19. Reserve estimates from *World Resources, 1990–91,* 320. Data on consumption and usage from *Statistical Abstract of the U.S.,* 1992; and *The World Almanac, 1992,* 192–193.

20. Natio nal Acid Precipitation Assessment Program (NAPAP), *Assessment Highlights* (Washington, D.C., 1991).

21. Figures on fuel wood consumption are from *Statistical Abstract of the U.S.,* 1992, table 950; and *Historical Statistics of the U.S.,* 1957, 355.

22. Paul R. Ehrlich and Anne H. Ehrlich, "The Most Overpopulated Nation," in Grant, ed., *Elephants in the Volkswagen,* 126.

23. Paul R. Ehrlich, Anne H. Ehrlich and John P. Holdven, *Ecoscience* (San Francisco: W. H. Freeman, 1977), 477.

24. For an interesting discussion of this problem, see Paul Werbos, "Energy and Population," in Grant, ed., *Elephants in the Volkswagen,* chap. 3.

25. "Space Photos Show Forests in Pacific Northwest Are in Peril, Scientists Say," *New York Times,* 11 June 1992.

26. *High Country News* (Paonia, Colo.), 29 January 1990, 3. This summary draws on the ongoing account in that journal, particularly the issues of 26 February and 17 December 1990; plus *Inner Voice,* the journal of AFSEEE (Eugene, Oreg.), and *New York Times,* 4 March 1990, 1.

27. *Sierra Magazine,* July–August 1992, 24–32.

28. *High Country News,* 21 September 1992, 5. The project has prepared extensive documentation of its charges. Inquiries should be addressed to Liz Sedler, Inventory Inquiry Project, P.O. Box 1203, Sandpoint, Idaho 83864; tel.: (208) 263-5281.

29. Report entitled "Management of Federal Timber Resources: The Loss of Accountability," available with a covering letter "Keeping Our Promises" dated 15 June 1992 from the Committee on Interior and Insular Affairs, U.S. House of Representatives, Washington, D.C. 20515.

30. Data on wood production and trade are from the FAO (U.N. Food and Agriculture Organization) "Agrostat" data base; and *Statistical Abstract of the U.S.,* various years. Because data on forestry are compiled slowly, "now" in these citations refers to the late 1980s. Note also that there has been considerable year-to-year fluctuation in per capita consumption, with a generally upward trend since 1975 (*Abstract,* 1992, table 1137).

31. Data are from the *Statistical Abstract of the U.S.*, 1962, 1992.

32. See Don Hinrichsen, "*Waldsterben:* Forest Death Syndrome," in *Amicus Journal*, Spring 1986, 23–27. The quotation concerning the United States is from NAPAP, *Assessment Highlights* (Washington, D.C., 1991).

33. "How Fast Can Trees Migrate?" *Science*, 10 February 1989, 735–737.

34. U.S. Water Resources Council, quoted by David Pimentel and Marcia Pimentel, *Land, Energy and Water: The Constraints Governing Ideal U.S. Population Size* (Teaneck, N.J.: Negative Population Growth, Inc., NPG Forum Series, January 1990).

35. Data from FAO, *Production Yearbooks*.

36. *Statistical Abstract of the U.S.*, 1992, 650.

37. *U.S.A. National Report*, 145. Detailed data are available in the USDA Soil Conservation Service, *Summary Report: 1987 National Resources Inventory* (Washington, D.C.: U.S. Government Printing Office, #1989-718-608, December 1989).

38. Worldwatch Institute, *Vital Signs* (New York: W. W. Norton, 1992), 40.

39. Tennenbaum and Costanza, "The Plight of the Chesapeake."

40. "Phosphate: Debate Over an Essential Resource," *Science*, 18 July 1980, 372.

41. Malin Falkenmark and Carl Widstrand, "Population and Water Resources: A Delicate Balance," *Population Bulletin* 47, no. 3 (November 1992): 13.

42. Pimentel and Pimentel, "Land, Energy and Water," 29. For the source of the estimate for crop losses to insects, see following note.

43. Waldemar Klassen, U.S. Department of Agriculture, to the Entomological Society of America, "Entomologists Wane as Insects Wax," *Science*, 10 November 1989, 754. At the same meeting, Dr. Robert Metcalf, University of Illinois, estimated that annual crop losses to insects alone (not counting other pathogens) rose from 7 percent in the 1940s to 13 percent in the 1980s.

44. L. B. Brattstein et al., "Insecticide Resistance: Challenge to Pest Management and Basic Research," *Science*, 14 March 1986, 1255.

45. "Moths Take the Field Against Biopesticide," *Science*, 1 November 1991, 646.

46. "Food Safety" (editorial), *Amicus Journal*, Summer 1987, 2. The study found sufficient data to undertake quantitative analysis on only 28 of the 300-plus pesticides licensed for use on food. A later EPA national pesticide survey of drinking water wells

found pesticide traces in 10 percent of community wells sampled and 4 percent of individual farm wells, though most of the contamination was below levels considered harmful to human health. For a discussion of the complex issues of pesticide threats, see *U.S.A. National Report*, 315–321.

47. USDA Soil Conservation Service, *Summary Report: 1987 National Resources Inventory*, table 13.

48. USDA Economic Research Service, *World Agriculture: Trends and Indicators, 1970–89*, Statistical Bulletin no. 815, September 1990, 512.

49. *Statistical Abstract of the U.S.*, 1992, 639.

50. Thomas Eisner, Cornell University, and Edward O. Wilson, Harvard University, at the 100th Annual Meeting of the Entomological Society of America. See also note 43.

51. News release from the Office of Science and Technology Policy, Executive Office of the President, 28 June 1983.

52. This was one conclusion of the oversight board for the NAPAP report published in February 1991. See *Science*, 19 April 1991, 371.

53. "Disappearing Mushrooms: Another Mass Extinction?" *Science*, 6 December 1991, 14–59.

54. "Jersey Fish Kill Stirs New Fears of Decline in Region's Waters," *New York Times*, 3 July 1988, 1.

55. "Red Menace in the World's Oceans," *Science*, 11 September 1992, 1476.

56. "Societies Sound Alarm on Biodiversity," *Science*, 14 August 1992, 876.

57. Associated Press, 30 April 1993, 01:31 EDT.

58. "Emerging Viruses, Emerging Threat," *Science*, 19 January 1990, 279.

59. "Antibiotics in Animal Feed Linked to Human Ills," *New York Times*, 22 February 1987, 1.

60. "TB Kills 13th Inmate in New York Prison System," *New York Times*, 17 November 1991, 20.

61. Reuters, London, 24 June 1993, 09:30, and 24 September 1993, 20:30.

62. "The Microbic Wars" (editorial), *Science*, 21 August 1992, 1021. (Reprinted by permission of *Science* magazine, copyright 1992 by the AAAS.)

63. For comparability, data from 1928 to 1947 have been interpolated to five-year figures. World data for 1990 are not yet available.

64. Emmett J. Horton and W. Dale Compton, "Technological Trends in Automobiles," *Science*, 10 August 1984, 591. The figures are for a compact vehicle, a Ford Escort.

65. C. D. Masters et al., "Resource Constraints in Petroleum Production Potential," *Science*, 12 July 1991, 147.

66. "Clean Thoughts on Clean Air," *Science*, 10 September 1993, 1371. (Reprinted by permission of *Science* magazine, copyright 1993 by the AAAS.)

67. For a fuller discussion of "optimum population," see Lindsey Grant, "Reconciling Texas and Berkeley," in Grant, ed., *Elephants in the Volkswagen*, chap. 1.

68. Michel Camdessus, press conference, 23 September 1993; Reuters, Washington, D.C., 23 September 1993.

69. Lawrence Summers, address to international business executives, 23 September 1993; quoted by Associated Press, 24 September 1993, 17:57 EDT.

70. Reuters, Bruges, Belgium, 23 September 1993, 10:22.

71. Associated Press, 9 April 1993, 02:10 EDT.

72. Testimony by Ronald E. Kutscher, Associate Commissioner, Bureau of Labor Statistics; Associated Press, 12 April 1993, 18:08 EDT.

73. "Price of Progress: 'Pre-engineering' Gives Firms New Efficiency, Workers the Pink Slip," *Wall Street Journal*, 16 March 1993, 1.

74. "Help Is on the Way for the Threatened Ozone Shield," *Science*, 1 January 1993, 28.

75. See "A Technical Fix for the Greenhouse," *Science*, 22 May 1992, 1144.

76. *U.S.A. National Report*, 197.

77. Werbos, "Energy and Population."

78. For a discussion of the processes of foresight, see Lindsey Grant, *Foresight and National Decisions: The Horseman and the Bureaucrat* (Lanham, Md.: University Press of America, 1988).

79. Detailed at length in Lindsey Grant, "The Cornucopian Fallacies," in Grant, ed., *Elephants in the Volkswagen*, chap. 11.

CHAPTER 2

1. "Census Reports It May Have Missed Up to 6.3 Million People," *Virginian-Pilot* (Norfolk, Va.), 19 April 1991, 3.

2. John M. Berry, "Experts Agree: Fixing the Economy Won't Be Easy," *Washington Post National Weekly Edition*, 7–13 September 1992, 8.

3. Campbell Gibson, "The Contribution of Immigration to the Growth and Ethnic Diversity of the American Population," paper presented at the biannual meeting of the American Philosophical Society, Philadelphia, 7 November 1991; see also Campbell Gib-

son, "The Contributions of Immigrants to the U.S. Population Growth: 1790–1970," *International Migration Review* 9 (Summer 1975): 157–176.

4. Jeffrey S. Passel and Barry Edmonston, *Immigration and Race: Recent Trends in Immigration to the United States* (Washington, D.C.: Urban Institute, 1992).

5. United Nations, *World Population Prospects 1992* (New York: U.N., 1992).

6. Peter Morrison, *Forecasting Population of Small Areas: An Overview* (Santa Barbara: Rand Corp., 1977).

7. For a more detailed discussion of recent Census Bureau projections, see Leon F. Bouvier and John L. Martin, "Four Hundred Million Americans! The Latest Census Bureau Projections," in *Backgrounder* (Washington, D.C., Center for Immigration Studies), January 1993.

8. U.S. Bureau of the Census, "Projections of the Population of the United States, by Age, Sex and Race: 1988 to 2080," *Current Population Reports*, P-25-1018 (Washington, D.C.: U.S. Government Printing Office, 1989).

9. Dennis A. Ahlburg and J. W. Vaupel, "Alternative Projections of the U.S. Population," *Demography* 27 (December 1990): 648.

10. Barry Edmonston and Jeffrey S. Passel, *The Future Immigrant Population of the United States* (Washington, D.C.: Urban Institute, 1992).

11. Leon F. Bouvier, *Peaceful Invasions: Immigration and Changing America* (Lanham, Md.: University Press of America, 1992).

12. U.S. Bureau of the Census, "Population Projections of the United States by Age, Sex, Race and Hispanic Origin: 1992 to 2050," *Current Population Reports*, P-25-1092 (Washington, D.C.: U.S. Government Printing Office, 1992).

13. U.S. Bureau of the Census, "Population Projections of the United States, by Age, Sex, Race and Hispanic Origin: 1993 to 2050," *Current Population Reports*, P-25-1104 (Washington, D.C.: U.S. Government Printing Office, September 1993).

14. Lindsey Grant, "What We Can Learn From the Missing Airline Passengers," *NPG Forum*, November 1992.

15. "How to Play the Asylum Game," *Newsweek*, 2 August 1993, 23.

16. Leon F. Bouvier, "Shifting Shares of the Population and U.S. Fertility," *Population and Environment*, September 1991, 24–43.

17. Bouvier, *Peaceful Invasions*, 38.

18. W. Parker Frisbie, *Trends in Ethnic Relations: Hispanics and Anglos* (Austin: Texas Research Center Papers, 1986), ser. 8, p. 1.

19. As cited in Scott McConnell, "The Battle over Immigration," *Fortune*, 9 May 1988, 94.

CHAPTER 3

1. "Effluent in Passaic River on Rise but Water Is Called Safe to Drink," *New York Times*, 25 January 1981, 1.

2. "New York City Is Under Pressure to Protect Its Precious Upstate Watershed," *New York Times*, 20 December 1992, 18Y.

3. *U.S.A. National Report*, 253.

4. Oral communication from SoCal Edison official, 22 February 1993.

5. U.S. Department of Agriculture, *World Agriculture, Trends and Indicators, 1970–89*, ERS Statistical Bulletin 815, September 1990, 514.

6. Dan Walters, "Growth Needs New Approach," *Sacramento Bee*, 1 January 1990, A12.

7. State Comprehensive Plan Committee, *Keys to Florida's Future: Winning in a Competitive World* (Tallahassee, 1987). It should be noted that the figures are even more shocking in 1992 than in 1987 and will be increasingly so in future years.

8. Bouvier and Weller, *Florida in the 21st Century*, 159–160.

9. *Statistical Abstract of the U.S.*, 1992, table 939.

10. This estimate is a ballpark figure for the average coal-fired steam plant, derived from information supplied orally by an officer of SoCal Edison (see note 4). This figure includes the interest on capital during construction, hooking into the grid and other highly variable costs that make a precise estimate very difficult. The plant itself, on a turnkey basis, might cost $1,100 to $1,200 per installed kilowatt. The comparable figure for a scaled-up version of the low-pollution "Cool Water" technology might be in the vicinity of $2,500.

11. Vernon M. Briggs, Jr., "Political Confrontation with Economic Reality," in Grant, ed., *Elephants in the Volkswagen*, 81.

12. Bureau of Labor Statistics, *Employment and Earnings* (January 1991), 170. The data are for the 20-to-24-year-old cohort.

CHAPTER 4

1. Otis L. Graham, Jr., testimony before the Joint Economic Committee of the U.S. Congress, June 1986, 16.

2. Pimentel and Pimentel, "Land, Energy and Water," 30.

3. Robert Costanza, "Balancing Humans in the Biosphere," in Grant, ed., *Elephants in the Volkswagen*, 50.

4. Werbos, "Energy and Population," 49.

5. Michael S. Teitelbaum and Jay M. Winter, *The Fear of Population Decline* (New York: Academic Press, 1985), 142.

6. John Weeks, "How to Influence Fertility: The Experience So Far," in Grant, ed., *Elephants in the Volkswagen*, 195. Much of this section is derived from Weeks's excellent paper.

7. U.S. Bureau of the Census, "Fertility of American Women: June 1990," *Current Population Reports*, P-20-454 (Washington, D.C.: U.S. Government Printing Office, 1991), table 4.

8. Cray Swicegood, F. D. Bean, E. H. Stephen and W. Opitz, "Language Usage and Fertility in the Mexican-Origin Population of the U.S.," *Demography* 25, no. 1 (1986): 30.

9. Census Bureau, "Fertility of American Women," table 5.

10. Linda Piccinino, Linda Peterson and William Pratt, "Unplanned Pregnancies in the United States, 1982–1988: What Are the Trends, What Are the Causes?" paper presented at the Population Association of America annual meeting, 1993.

11. Weeks, "How to Influence Fertility," 195.

12. See, for example, *Earth in the Balance*, pt. 3.

13. For a summary of such polls, see Bouvier, *Peaceful Invasions*, 196.

14. Dan Stein, "Why America Needs a Moratorium on Immigration," *Social Contract*, Fall 1992, 55.

15. Tom Morganthau, "America: Still a Melting Pot?" *Newsweek*, 9 August 1993, 18.

16. "The Rekindled Flame," *Wall Street Journal*, 3 July 1990, A10.

17. Malcolm Gladwell and Rachel E. Stassen-Berger, "Building a Human Highway: U.S. Policy and Labor Needs Abet the Influx of Chinese Immigrants," *Washington Post National Weekly Edition*, 21–27 June 1993, 32.

18. David Simcox, "Sustainable Immigration: Learning to Say No," in Grant, ed., *Elephants in the Volkswagen*, 172.

CHAPTER 5

1. Summary volume titled *Population and the American Future* (Bergenfield, N. J.: The New American Library, 1972).

2. Grant, *Elephants in the Volkswagen*, 9–11.

3. Phillip Longman, "We're in the Tax Revolt Zone," *Florida Trend*, October 1992, 18.

4. Robert Reich, "The Real Enemy," *Atlantic Monthly*, February 1991, 43.

5. Population Reference Bureau, "Where Will the Next 50 Million Americans Live?" *Population Bulletin*, October 1971, 30.

6. Dick Marlowe, "Study: Orlando Has Bright Future," *Orlando Sentinel*, "Central Florida Business" sec., 28 December 1992, 3.

7. Lincoln Day, "What Will a ZPG Society Be Like?" *Population Bulletin* 33, no. 3 (June 1978): 37.

8. George Kennan, *Around the Cragged Hill: A Political and Personal Philosophy* (New York: W. W. Norton, 1993), 100.

9. *Population and the American Future*, 6.

10. Cited in Michael Kernan, "Growing Up with the Bomb," *Washington Post*, 20 November 1983, L1.

11. A recent example is a major survey sponsored by foundations supporting Hispanic organizations: it found that 75.2 percent of non-Hispanic Whites thought there are too many immigrants, while the proportion among different groups of Hispanics holding the same opinion varied from 65.5 percent to 79.4 percent; *USA Today*, 16 December 1992.

12. Arthur Schlesinger, Jr., "The Cult of Ethnicity, Good or Bad," *Time*, 8 July 1991, 21.

13. Pat Truly, "U.S. Drifts Without Shared Purpose," *Ft. Worth Star-Telegram*, 24 August 1993, 12.

14. John Gray, "No Nation Is Indivisible," *New York Times Book Review*, 27 December 1992, 7.

15. Amitai Etzioni, *The Spirit of Community* (New York: Crown Publishers, 1993), 25.

16. Michael Lerner, "What I Mean by 'The Politics of Meaning,'" *Washington Post National Weekly Edition*, 21–27 June 1993, 24.

17. The Global Tomorrow Coalition (1325 G Street N.W., Washington, D.C. 20005) was created by a consortium of environmental and population groups to follow up on the *Global 2000 Report*, and the single policy proposal to which it is formally committed is the creation of improved foresight machinery in the government. A parallel proposal was part of the *Blueprint for the Environment*, a series of policy proposals drawn up by a wide array of environmentalists, organized by a coalition of 17 major environmental groups chaired by the National Wildlife Federation, and presented to President-elect Bush in 1988.

18. See Grant, *Foresight and National Decisions*, for a detailed discussion of the concept of foresight and a description and critique of the Critical Trends Assessment Act and other legislative and executive-branch proposals for improved foresight.

19. U.S. Council on Environmental Quality and Department of State, *The Global 2000 Report to the President: Entering the 21st*

Century, Gerald O. Barney, Study Director (Washington, D.C.: U.S. Government Printing Office, 3 vols., 1980).

20. U.S. Council on Environmental Quality and Department of State, *Global Future: Time to Act* (Washington, D.C.: U.S. Government Printing Office, January 1981), 11.

INDEX